Monday Night Wars
A Fans Side of the Story

G.G. Conte

ISBN: 1540762653
ISBN-13: 978-1540762658

DEDICATION

This is dedicated to every wrestling fan around the world. The fans that enjoy the art of wrestling, both in and out of the ring. It's also dedicated to the wrestlers and crew who help bring that art to us on a daily basis.

This is also dedicated to my grandmother, who passed away during the writing of this book. She will always be my number one fan.

"In order to be the man, you have to beat the man."

Ric Flair

"You sit there, and you thump your Bible, and you say your prayers, and it didn't get you anywhere. Talk about your Psalms, talk about John 3:16 - AUSTIN 3:16 SAYS I JUST WHIPPED YOUR ASS!"

Stone Cold Steve Austin

CHAPTER I
TBS

What is Professional Wrestling? Is it fake? Is it real? To tell you the truth, it's both. Yes, what happens on-screen is entirely predetermined with the winners decided beforehand. However, the world behind the curtains, the glitz, and the glamour, is a world that is just as real as any other sport and just as political as one as well.

In the midst of that realism was a war between what were then, the two largest companies in the entire sport of Professional Wrestling; *The Monday Night Wars*, which pitted Vince McMahon's WWF (WWE currently) and Ted Turner's WCW.

In a span of six years, these two companies would go head-to-head on Monday Nights, with WWF's *Monday Night Raw* and WCW's *Monday Night Nitro* both featured in identical prime-time slots. But the big question that seems to invade the minds of all wrestling fans that were around during this time is how the hell this war got started and why did the war end the way it did?

This would all begin in 1983 with Vince McMahon Jr.'s purchase of Capital Sports, the parent company of the WWF. He would purchase this company from his own father, with his father not truly knowing his sons intent with the company, to take the company national.

McMahon's attempt to go national was not met with immediate success as some within the WWE would lead you to believe. Purchasing Georgia Championship Wrestling was McMahon's attempt to turn the tide and try to appeal to a mass audience as the purchase meant a timeslot on Ted Turner's TBS, which was a network broadcasting mainly in the southeast at the time, a territory that was then unfamiliar to the WWF.

However, this venture would not last long as many of the southeast wrestling fans did not take well to McMahon's style of wrestling, which was more cartoonish when compared to the more traditional wrestling style of GCW. It is actually really unclear what words were said between McMahon and Turner as ratings were sinking for wrestling on TBS with McMahon guiding the ship.

The only side of the story that has seemed to be heard has been McMahon's, in which there was a meeting between the two and McMahon basically backed out of their contract as he could not work with Turner and would sell GCW to Jim Crockett Jr. for a sum of one million dollars, which Crockett explained as being the money that funded the very first *Wrestlemania*. It's unclear how accurate Crockett is but it's pretty understandable as *Wrestlemania* would debut less than a year later.

It doesn't come as a surprise that McMahon's venture with TBS was a failure. I know many fans that weren't around for that era tend to think that it should have been an immediate success but it was a far different industry back in the 80s'. McMahon's journey to take the WWF national was viewed by many territories to be wrestling's version of sacrilege. It was an industry that was territorial with each territory allowed to operate independently without fear of competition from others.

In fact, each promotion would sometimes work together to help the other, if the other were needing help, for instance, they would transfer some of their stars to that promotion briefly to help draw a crowd.

McMahon wanted to end the territorial reign of wrestling as he a saw more national appeal in the product then the rest of his peers. McMahon was so obsessed with going national that he continued after the failure of the GCW purchase un-phased as he would continue acquiring other territories and their stars. The WWF's fast expansion into other parts of the country began to collapse many of the territories to the point where they had no choice but to sell their companies to McMahon.

However, the unfortunate flip-side to this was that WWF's growth also saw movement from Atlanta's territory, World Championship Wrestling. With other territories dying on the southeast, fans on that side of the country refused to watch McMahon's product and turned to WCW.

However, while WCW's growth was slow, WWF's seemed to be happening at an uncontrollable rate. McMahon would make a deal with the then brand new network, Music Television (MTV), and bring wrestling into a realm that was then unknown to the world of Professional Wrestling, including wrestlers in music videos and having popular musicians on their shows. MTV would also broadcast the very first live wrestling match on cable television.

This would infamously lead to McMahon's most ambitious venture on March 1, 1985, *Wrestlemania*. *Wrestlemania* was broadcast on pay-per-view in select areas and would reach over one million viewers on Closed-Circuit Television, making it the biggest wrestling success story at that period in time.

While the show, in retrospect, was unbelievably terrible from a pure wrestling standpoint, it definitely has earned its place in history and helped launch the WWF to great heights.

WWF would see more success as their ratings on syndicated television would begin to rise and the creation of the *King of the Ring*.

Jim Crockett would attempt to compete, with the promotion under the name NWA World Championship Wrestling. Crockett saw the need to also go national in 1986, purchasing many of the remaining territories, including some unassociated with the NWA. This would lead to *Starrcade*, which would be WCW's attempt to compete with McMahon's *Wrestlemania*.

In my view, Crockett's attempt was very understandable. It was either compete or die at that point as McMahon was gaining so much clout in the wrestling industry and a lot of control over the cable and pay-per-view networks.

Crockett promoted the hell out of *Starrcade*, to the point that it should have been an unbelievable success, worthy of competing on McMahon's level. Its card was superior to the first *Wrestlemania* in terms of wrestling quality and the promotion under TBS was notable too as TBS was beginning to grow as well. However, these attempts would backfire on Crockett as McMahon's power over the pay-per-view industry would override *Starrcade*. McMahon countered *Starrcade* with his newly created event, *Survivor Series*.

McMahon would threaten the pay-per-view providers with no *Wrestlemania* to those who carried *Starrcade* over Survivor Series. Seeing that *Wrestlemania* was one of the biggest moneymakers at the time for pay-per-view, over eighty percent of the providers pulled out of carrying *Starrcade*.

Many might see this as a dirty tactic by McMahon, but from a business standpoint, it made a lot of sense. Given McMahon's position and his want for his company to succeed, this was a vital move he had to make to keep his competition at bay. *Survivor Series* would garner a 7.0 buyrate to *Starrcade's* 3.30. While still a great number by WCW standards at the time, it was undoubtedly damaged by McMahon.

The financial failure of *Starrcade* would lead to huge financial problems for Crockett's promotion, which would lead to his sale of the promotion to Ted Turner on October 11, 1988. Turner had been positioning himself on buying the company for some time. Turner would then rename the promotion as World Championship Wrestling. This sale would be crucial for the survival of the company, as Turner was more than interested in competing with McMahon.

CHAPTER II
Slow Rise and Quick Downslide of WCW

Ted Turner was not only a fan of wrestling but enjoyed having it on his network because it was an inexpensive product to have and was perfect for a younger network like his TBS.

For the first couple of years under Turner's ownership, the company saw an upward slide in profits, with Ric Flair placed as head booker and also made World Champion once again during this time.

Flair's reign, at the beginning, was the only option that he had. While wrestlers booking themselves as champions is never really well-received, Flair didn't have much of a choice. There wasn't a lot of established talent in WCW that could carry that torch and Flair was already viewed in high esteem then, so it made sense for him to be on top.

In his reign, he would have classic matches with Ricky Steamboat, who was one of the best in-ring workers of all time.

However, by 1990, Flair's reign was beginning to last way too long, even for fans, as WCW's profits began to take another hit. To add insult to injury, the behind-the-scenes of the company were also falling to shreds as wrestlers began to complain about Flair's role as head booker and naming himself as champion.

Flair would then be released as head booker and replaced by Ole Anderson. Anderson as booker was another problem. I'm sure it seemed like a good idea because you had someone who was very knowledgeable of wrestling, not only from an in-ring standpoint but a business standpoint, having been around longer than Flair. The issue, was that he was someone who saw his older wrestling friends on top rather than younger, up-and-coming wrestlers.

So essentially, you have someone who is actually similar to Flair from a booking perspective but instead of himself, he booked his friends on top. The big coo in this was that one of his friends, at the time, was Ric Flair. So, despite the wrestlers petitions to get Flair out of the role of head booker, so they could see a rise in their careers, their move actually assisted Flair more.

By 1990, the company was experiencing record lows in attendance and house shows were dwindling to only a couple hundred tickets sold and the rest being given away for free. Anderson also saw fit to try and emulate WWF's product with more glitz and glamour to make the product more mainstream. All attempts were unbelievable failures.

It was in this dilemma that WCW permanently distanced itself from NWA, therefore operating as its own company.

There was a problem with this because WCW and NWA recognized Flair as their champion well into 1991. WCW would appoint Jim Herd as the president at that point. Herd was made president due to his, so-called, experience in television. I don't necessarily see how being head of a local St. Louis television station and manager of a Pizza Hut gives you knowledge of a national televised show and company, but I digress.

There was early animosity between Flair and Herd. Herd saw an easy way to get the championship off of Flair and that was firing him just before the *Great American Bash* event in 1991. From what I can gather, Herd tried to be business-like with renegotiating Flair's contract and appearing to be very cordial about it. But it was clear that his offers were meant to be put in a way where Flair would reject them.

You didn't have to be a huge wrestling insider to know that Herd wanted Flair out of the company and stripped of the title. Despite how unethical his efforts were, it's tough to argue against Herd's reasoning. He was made president of a company that was dying under

Flair and Anderson. One of the two had to be removed in order for Herd to restore some order within the company. Was his efforts in poor taste and could he have planned it better? Yes, but in the world of business, you sometimes have to play that unfair card in order to win.

Yes, Ric Flair was the company's biggest draw but that isn't saying much when your company is not selling a lot of tickets.

Despite this change within the company, order was not restored in WCW. In fact, they quickly began to get worse. While Herd had some wrestling knowledge, having broadcast wrestling on his previous station, he didn't have great long-term creative knowledge of the business, which was very noticeable going into 1992. Storylines were shorter and characters were being poorly developed.

It was in this predicament that Herd was released and replaced by Kip Allen Frey. Frey had no wrestling knowledge but seemed like a good fit for the company as he was a good businessman and was good with finances. Financial savior was exactly what WCW needed on the business side of things. They were a company that was losing millions per year.

Fay turned out to be more of a thorn in

WCW as he would incorporate bonuses to wrestlers. I guess he felt that WCW should be run like other businesses and award good employees. While extremely generous of him, WCW was not in a position to where bonuses could be awarded. Seeing this financial debacle, Fay was quickly released only months into his term and replaced by wrestling veteran, Bill Watts.

Watts seemed like the perfect fit for the role, he had perfect wrestling knowledge and the business mind to see that cuts had to be made. So, this means everything should be fixed right? Wrong. Watts, while knowledgeable, was more interested in cutting back the product so much, that it looked like it was based in the 70s'. Lighting was cut back so much in the arena's that crowds could not be seen and wrestlers were no longer allowed to use top-rope maneuvers, making wrestlers like Brian Pillman less useful in the ring.

In retrospect, Bill Watts was just trying to make WCW what it was to him when he was wrestling. However, in a new generation, it was now a completely obsolete way of handling business. With WWF producing high-quality television, from a production standpoint, it made WCW look the darker of the two.

Bill Watts did make budget cuts, but

not in the areas where they were needed. His form of management actually wound up spending more than what he was cutting and it had everything to do with their travel expenses and house shows. Watts and others in management roles at WCW were under the impression that if they did more house shows, it would make up for the lack of tickets they were selling.

The pressure was coming down on management from wrestlers, Turner Broadcasting, and Hank Aaron of all people. Aaron might seem like someone out of left field (no pun intended) but Watts didn't do WCW any favors when he made racial remarks towards Aaron, who was with the Braves, who were also with Turner Broadcasting. When you're with a company that was as big as Turner Broadcasting, it's best to keep personal opinions to yourself. Unfortunately, Watts did not believe in this.

With so much pressure on him, Watts would resign from WCW himself.

Vince McMahon and the WWF couldn't have asked for more success in the 80s'. With *Wrestlemania* riding high, numerous pay-per-view ventures, and syndication on the USA Network, the WWF was reaching levels of success unknown in the wrestling world.

While still not gaining a whole lot of support from the southeast, they had managed to gain recognition not only from the rest of the US but also a global market that WWE still retains to this day.

1987 is considered by many to be the peak of what would be called *The Golden Era* of wrestling. *Wrestlemania III* would become the largest event of that era, attracting a reported 93,000 fans at the Pontiac Silverdome and featuring the classic match between Hulk Hogan and Andre the Giant.

However, the WWF was also becoming known for its younger stars as well, as their tag team division would see the biggest expansion during this era and would play a major role in the company's successful mid-card roster.

WWF's ratings and PPV buyrate success would remain consistent through the late 80s' with wrestlers like Hulk Hogan, The Ultimate

Warrior, Randy Savage, and more guiding the ship.

It also helped that their biggest attraction, Hulk Hogan, had become so mainstream that he ventured into other realms of entertainment, which helped put eyes on wrestling as well.

But all eras reach an end at some point. When 1990 came rolling around, it was becoming very evident that there was a need to change things around. While Hogan was still their biggest name, the crowds were slowly beginning to reject his character as his matches were becoming more and more one-dimensional.

Wrestlemania VI would be used to mark a new era for the WWF, with Hulk Hogan appearing to pass the torch to The Ultimate Warrior. *Wrestlemania VI* was an unbelievable success but business continued to steadily decline from their once great heights.

By 1991, while WWF was still drawing good numbers, media scrutiny began to surface over the WWF. McMahon would face charges over distributing steroids to his wrestlers.

The trial would not be a quick one, as the WWF would continue with business as usual and the trial would need another three years to get going.

In the meantime, McMahon tried to right the ship of the WWF, which continued to see a decline. In by no means were the declines as substantial as WCW's but in the WWF's current state, small declines meant millions of dollars to them, and as a private company that was a huge loss.

1992 was seen, at the time, to be WWF's biggest chance to rebound. Ric Flair, who had been let go by WCW over contract negotiation disagreements, had signed on to the WWF. Despite primarily being featured in the south, Flair was known worldwide, with many fans of the WWF recognizing him and knowing his legendary status.

Ric Flair generated huge feedback for WWF as he would appear on-screen with WCW's World Championship, a move that would be seen again in the future by WCW, but we'll get to that later. This caused an uproar from WCW, who sued Flair. This is also a common misconception, WWF was not the one sued over the incident, it was Flair.

Flairs argument was that he was still owed his deposit ($25,000) for the belt. WCW would eventually pay Flair his deposit, adding ten thousand in interest. The only order made against the WWF was to block out the belt in any footage shot.

In order to keep interest around Flair,

Flair would win the 1992 *Royal Rumble*, therefore winning the WWF title. This was supposed to be the big setup for Flair vs. Hogan for *Wrestlemania VIII*.

The WWF built up so much interest around this match but, for whatever reason, Vince McMahon decided not to go through with the match. Hogan and Flair would then be assigned different matches with Hogan facing Sid Justice (someone who shouldn't have been anywhere near the main event scene at the time) and Ric Flair facing Randy Savage.

While *Wrestlemania VIII* was a good event in its own right with Flair and Savage putting on a classic match, the main event couldn't help but feel forced. Justice was not main event material at the time and nowhere near Hogan's level. To make matters worse, Hogan's crowd reactions were starting to taper off quite a bit, which didn't help the match.

There have been nonstop rumors as to why WWF pulled out of the Flair/Hogan match and we can really only go based on WWF's word, which should be taken with a grain of salt. Their reasoning was that they had tried a few attempts with Hogan and Flair at their house shows, which didn't generate the numbers they were expecting.

From my standpoint, it had to do with the

crowd's reactions to Flair. WWF was still trying to present Hogan as the top face, despite an obvious backlash from some of the audience. I think there was a fear of Flair coming out the better of the two, whether he won or lost the match, so they needed to pit him against someone where the crowd reaction was not as big of an issue. That's only my opinion and I'm sticking to it.

By mid-1992, WWF began to incorporate smaller wrestlers into the main event scene. Bret Hart, Mr. Perfect (Curt Hennig), Shawn Michaels, and Davey Boy Smith would see huge pushes that year. None were bigger than Hart's push as he would be set out to win the title from Flair on October 12, 1992. Hart's push would pay dividends to WWF's future only a couple years later.

However, despite a slight turnaround in business due to the introduction of new, younger stars and some help from Flair's appearance, the media attention around the WWF and the upcoming steroid trial were still hovering heavily over the WWF. As the dates grew closer, WWF's business continued to see decline going into 1993.

WWF's then primetime show, *Prime Time Wrestling*, was struggling in the ratings and canceled by USA Network. WWF would use this to revamp the product, replacing *Prime*

Time Wrestling with *Monday Night Raw*. With *Raw*, as a cost saver, they would broadcast the show within the Grand Ballroom at Manhattan Studios.

The initial concept of the show was to be a sixty-minute live show every Monday night but with WWF being a private company at the time, this would prove to be financially impossible to sustain. They would then decide to pre-tape many of the shows, while only going live occasionally, usually after a pay-per-view.

Raw proved to be a huge success for the company and was revolutionary for its time as live pro wrestling was not common on cable television.

However, while the show itself was successful, the WWF was still struggling from a creative standpoint. The first half of 1993 was a business nightmare for WWF as Hulk Hogan would play a huge role on how his departure from the WWF would be. Hogan had decided to part ways from the WWF in 1993 but apparently didn't want to leave without stirring up some major controversy first.

It was becoming clear that McMahon was looking to change his company's image, going from the larger than life characters to smaller, more athletic wrestlers. One of the wrestlers that McMahon saw as the next big draw was

Canadian wrestler, Bret Hart. Hart is now labeled arguably the best technical wrestler in the history of the business and he was already earning that reputation then.

With *Wrestlemania IX* approaching and Hogan already well publicized about leaving the WWF, they needed a transition from the aging star Hogan to the rising star Hart. So it seemed inevitable that Hogan and Hart would compete in a match. The match at *Wrestlemania IX* was set to be Hart vs. Yokozuna. The storyline was originally conceived to be Yokozuna winning the World Title from Hart by cheating and Hogan coming to win it from Yokozuna only minutes after that match had taken place.

It was a stupid idea, but it was originally said to all lead to Hogan's last match with WWF at *Summerslam*, losing the belt to Hart.

Everything went according to plan at *Wrestlemania IX* but fell apart after that. Hogan flat out refused to lose to Hart, as he felt that he wasn't in the same league as him, which seems to be Hogan's excuse to everything when it involves him losing. He would instead drop the belt to Yokozuna at *Summerslam*.

While Hart would eventually win the title back, it did leave a horrible black mark for the WWF that year as it was the only storyline that seemed to draw any attention from 1993. Hogan would not be seen on WWF television again for nine years after that.

If there was ever a year that WWF needed to be creatively on their game, it was 1993 because just as fans began to turn away from the product, the steroid trial seemed to become more of a topic.

The trial would finally commence on July 7, 1994. At a time when the WWF was already experiencing a financial decline, this only seemed to make matters worse.

The basis of the trial was that it was believed that Vince McMahon was distributing steroids to his wrestlers. A lot of people now believe the trial was just over the use of steroids in wrestling, which is incorrect; it was based on distribution on McMahon's part. The prosecution had to make the charges in that manner because, by law, they could not convict McMahon if he advised or recommended his wrestlers to use steroids, advising or recommending is not a crime in this case because it's still up to the individual to use them and they're the ones that get in trouble. The only way that McMahon could serve jail time would be if he distributed. The testimony that the prosecution was waiting for was from Hulk Hogan. Hogan had been ordered to testify for the case. Up until

Hogan's testimony, there hadn't been any proof of distribution on McMahon's part.

The prosecution was well aware of the media attention this was getting and conveniently kept Hogan as one of the last ones to testify. After all of the testimonies were in, including Hogan's, there was nothing to link McMahon to distributing the steroids, so all charges were dropped.

What should have been a huge win for McMahon and the WWF was a near company crusher, because despite the win in court, many of the wrestlers had admitted to using steroids themselves and that confession alone cast a dark shadow over the entire wrestling world, and kept a lot of parents from bringing their kids back to the shows.

WWF, from the viewer's standpoint, moved on with their touring and television broadcast as normal, but the behind-the-scenes of the company were in financial ruin and would need a complete overhaul to recover.

Chapter IV
Eric Bischoff Steps Up

With WWF under financial stress, it seemed like the perfect opportunity for WCW to capitalize. The capitalization was slow on their part. With Bill Watts stepping down, the position of Executive Producer was placed up for grabs for someone to take. By experience levels, the job seemed almost completely fit for Jim Ross, who seemed to be the next-in-line after Watts.

Jim Ross, who is one of the best commentators in wrestling, already had over twenty years under his belt in the wrestling business and seemed like an obvious pick. However, Ted Turner and Turner president, Bill Shaw, needed someone different for the role; someone who would not treat the company as a strictly southern promotion.

This person was Eric Bischoff. Bischoff had been hired on as a third tier announcer in WCW but had prior sales and commentating experience from the American Wrestling Alliance. Bischoff had much experience in business in general, which is what Turner and Shaw wanted.

Bischoff, who put his name on the list for potential candidates for the position, was promoted to Executive Producer in early 1993.

Bischoff's promotion would cause a longtime rivalry between Jim Ross and himself. Ross, who once was supervisor over Bischoff, didn't like the fact that he was now answering to him.

Jim Ross would go on to say for many years that he was fired by Bischoff. Bischoff has rebutted this statement in saying that he merely asked for his resignation once he found out about Bischoff being in the Executive Producer role. Instead of Bischoff allowing Jim Ross to be miserable with WCW's decision, he told Bill Shaw just to accept his resignation.

It seems easier to side with Ross' side of the story, as he has become so beloved over the years, but Bischoff sounds the more honest out of the two. I think there was just bitterness on Ross' end because he had been with the company for so long and probably felt overlooked when someone with less experience than him got the Executive Producer role. Hell, had it been me in the same position I would probably feel the same way.

The reason why Bischoff was hated so much right from the get-go was the fact that, as Executive Producer, he was pretty much in control of everything.

WCW was not run like a normal business. Its two real heads, which were Turner and Shaw, didn't look over the company 24/7.

They were far too busy for that. They would definitely see the product from time-to-time, Turner, more often than not, but they couldn't devote all of their time into the product as I'm sure they would have liked to. So, under those circumstances, they needed someone to be the figurehead of the company, and to oversee all of its proceedings.

This was one of the reasons why the company was such a failure for so long in Turner's first few years because there wasn't a great sense of control. Everyone before Bischoff thought about themselves and their friends, rather than the rest of the crew.

Bischoff had several different plans for the company but unfortunately didn't have the resources to put them to work immediately, which led to a pretty uneventful first year for WCW under Bischoff's reign.

His biggest deterrents were Dusty Rhodes and Ole Anderson, who were still in charge of booking and creative, which meant more cartoonish and kid-friendly programming, something that Bischoff was opposed to. Rhodes and Anderson were also notorious for fast and pointless feuds. Wrestlers like Sting and Cactus Jack (Mick Foley) were thrown from feud to feud, sometimes without warning or build up. They even had a brief feud with each other that went nowhere.

It also doesn't help that some of the between match segments were awful. The one that always gets the attention is the Shockmaster. WCW had recently signed Fred Ottman (formerly Tugboat in the WWF) and wanted to charge up his character and make him an intimidating heel. In WCW at the time, an intimidating heel apparently meant a puffy leather vest, jeans, and a glitter covered Star Wars Stormtrooper helmet.

Even if the segment had gone as planned, I can't imagine anyone who would have taken that character seriously. The segment ended up being one the most laughable things on television. Sting introduced him and instead of smashing through the wall, he trips and his helmet flies off.

I'm surprised Dusty Rhodes and Ole Anderson weren't fired then because that segment alone wasn't worth keeping them over.

With Bischoff though, he steadily pushed them out instead of actually throwing them out because it was apparent that they would leave anyway because neither wanted to work with him, Rhodes in particular, who viewed Bischoff along the lines that Ross did.

1994 would be the year when Bischoff started putting his ideas into action. The first thing on his list was to cut cost anywhere he could. WCW was a cash drain. It was losing ten million dollars or more a year and needed a turnaround.

One of Bischoff's first ideas was one that got him much resentment and that was ending all house shows. Old school pro wrestlers were used to house shows because wrestling is a business that's always on the road. This especially held true for the WWF, where their wrestlers were on the road over three-hundred days a year.

Because it was such a financial drain on the company's budget, Bischoff did not see the reason to keep traveling, when they weren't generating a profit from it in the first place.

His next move was to change the way they handled their production. Instead of performing in low lit, grungy, and empty seated arena's, they would move their Saturday show permanently to the Disney/MGM Studios. They booked one of the studio's soundstages and would film the show in front of a couple hundred tourists.

This idea was reviled by most within the company because it went against conventional logic within the industry. Conventional logic would think that a wrestling show should be performed in front of thousands of screaming fans in an arena, not in front of a couple hundred tourists, many of which are not wrestling fans and have to be told when to cheer and boo.

While this might have seemed against that sort of logic, WCW wasn't necessarily a company meeting that logic anyway. They weren't a wrestling show attracting thousands of people in an arena and didn't have legions of screaming fans, they needed something that would be fresh and new for them and would appeal more to a mass audience.

To keep cost down, the show would never be live, and there would be several shows taped at once. While a good idea from a financial standpoint on paper, it was a problem for the first year or so because wrestlers would need to walk out with titles that they might not win until a couple months after the taping of the show.

To combat this and keep fans from finding out ahead of time of title changes, they would have the wrestlers walking out with titles but it wouldn't be the one winning the title at all. This created a lot more confusion, so they just eventually stopped walking out with titles period and the show would eventually feature wrestlers that were not big enough names for titles.

The move to the Disney/MGM Studios, in my opinion, was one of the better ideas Bischoff had in his early years with the company. While it did force a lot of wrestlers to move to Orlando, Florida for a while, it was the best thing he could have come up with to keep cost down while still continuing to produce a WCW product on television.

It was also a major shift in production value. While it was a cheaper show overall to produce when compared to their productions in the bigger arenas, it was a much better-looking show. The soundstage was a much better lit, cleaner, and more production-friendly facility than the arena's that they were filming in prior.

With the new, better looking Saturday show filming at the Disney/MGM Studios, Bischoff and Flair set out to recruit Hulk Hogan.

There are many stories surrounding WCW's signing of Hogan. Many say it was Ric Flair that helped bring him in, some say it was Bischoff, and others say it was the both of them. Whichever is more accurate will probably never be known, but one thing was for sure, this was a big deal for WCW at the time.

While it was contradictory to what WCW was trying to do, because it would cost them a lot of money to bring him in, they needed a name to carry the brand they were trying to convey.

While Ric Flair and Sting were big names in their own right, they needed a mainstream name to really push them to a level of popularity that was unknown to the company then.

Because of Hogan's name, Bischoff really wanted to show that this was a big deal and turned Hogan's signing to WCW into a media frenzy. They even held a huge parade filled with Hogan fans for the contract signing. Hogan came down in a car during the parade that led to a stage where he would sign the contract.

In the wrestling industry and any business in general, contract signings are held in private. It's always between the boss and employee, no one else. So by making this a public event, it added to the magnitude of the whole situation.

This also marked one of the very few times contracts, guaranteed contracts for that matter, were ever brought up in the wrestling business. That's another thing people often forget because contracts are now required in companies like the WWE and even TNA, but there weren't a lot of guaranteed contracts in the wrestling business at the time.

Yes, if you were a big name and a company wanted to keep you for them and them only, they went through contracts.

However, if you were an up-and-comer or even just a jobber in the business, you usually worked based on a handshake and your salary was based on certain scenarios. For instance, your placement on the card, your performance, or you received a small percentage of the total revenue made for the show.

The reason why the wrestling industry worked like this for so long was because all of the wrestling companies back then were privately owned companies. These were not public companies, so they could only pay based on what they made and were much more tied down by budget constraints.

WCW was a company attached to a large public company, which differentiated it from other wrestling companies, such as its main competitor the WWF. Instead of being its own solo company, it was the product of Turner Broadcasting. This made budget and contracts much easier for them. One thing that should be pointed out about WCW's guaranteed contracts, was that while they were attached to WCW's overall budget, they weren't made out under WCW's name; they were contracts made out to Turner Broadcasting, which would all belong to AOL Time Warner in the end.

It was also that financial backing from

Turner that made the signing of Hogan a lot easier for Bischoff and Flair. During that time, as long as they had Turner's consent, they were golden.

With that being said, I still think that signing Hogan on June 11, 1994, was one of the dumbest mistakes they made. I'm not talking about what happened later on in the company, I'm talking about that point in time for WCW.

While Hogan was and still is a big name in the world of wrestling, signing him didn't make a whole lot of sense. Bischoff was trying to change the company's image for the better and turn it into a watchable wrestling show.

Hogan's reputation at the time was heavily damaged. He was still in severe damage control after the steroid trial with Vince McMahon and was not viewed in the high regard as he had been in the past.

Also, because of the steroid trial, a good chunk of the fans that were watching wrestling before then, were no longer watching after it was all over. While Hogan's signing was popular to see in person, it didn't really translate on television well, which was evident as the ratings didn't really move much with him on the roster.

Also, a problem was Hogan's demands. While he couldn't necessarily bully McMahon around, Hogan was smart enough to know he had it made with WCW and knew what he could get away with. He demanded creative control, a set salary, and limited appearances on WCW programming. While the latter would eventually be lifted a couple years later, the former on that list would be the most important to Hogan.

One of the main things Bischoff wanted to check off of his bucket list with Hogan was the dream match that WWF failed to pull off and that was Hogan facing Flair.

Hogan's debut match with WCW took place on July 17, 1994 at WCW's new event, *Bash at the Beach*. This was an important event not only for Bischoff, but for the entire company. This needed to be a success. Bischoff promoted the hell out of *Bash at the Beach* and wanted to make sure that the dream match between Hogan and Flair was in front of as many eyes as possible. He went as far as to label the match the *dream match*.

The event was a huge draw; it drew 14,000 fans, the largest turn out for a WCW event in years and drew their highest pay-per-view buyrate since their very first *Starrcade*.

Hogan would win the WCW World Title in his very first match with the company, which made sense given the hype his character had received since his contract signing. However, I was never a fan of Hogan winning the rematch between the two at *Halloween Havoc* the same year. I think that match should have gone to Flair, but that's just my opinion.

Don't get me wrong, I have nothing against Hogan as an entertainer and when it comes to promos, he's one of the best and most intense. When Hogan was in his prime in the 80s', he understood the entertainment aspect of the business. As the 90s' rolled around though, he was very self-aware on how big his name was and wanted to remain in the top spot, even if it meant pushing down those who deserved it more.

This was and still is nothing new in the wrestling world. There have been plenty of top performers that have been unwilling to give up their top status. However, for WCW, they were a company that didn't really need somebody like that under their watch.

For Hogan, I think in his mind, he could see the changing of the guard happening in the wrestling world. It was a world that was no longer dominated by giants and over-muscular athletes; it was now a sport where the smaller guys could now excel in and Hogan was someone that wanted wrestling to remain the way it was.

Shortly after his signing, Hogan worked with Bischoff on getting Randy Savage over to the company. Savage's contract was coming up in WWF and McMahon was slowly working Savage farther and farther away from in-ring activity. McMahon wanted to take the WWF in a new direction and unfortunately, that direction didn't include Savage and so he had Savage as a regular color commentator on *Raw* and some of the pay-per-views.

While Savage was an awesome color commentator, he obviously didn't see himself in that role. Savage, being a professional, stuck out the tenure of his contract with the WWF and formed a deal with WCW shortly afterward.

I honestly liked Savage's move to WCW more than Hogan's. Savage was still a great athlete and a much better in-ring performer than Hogan, in my opinion. With so much left in the tank, it didn't make sense for him to not be in the ring. So, his move to WCW was one that I enjoyed and I think it was a smart move on his part.

With that being said, Savage did also have access to a similar deal that Hogan had, which was a problem but he had a lot more professionalism than Hogan from my point-of-view.

While the signings of Hogan and Savage did bring WCW both good and bad criticism, it did attract attention, which I think was

Bischoff's ultimate goal. He didn't care if it was good or bad press, it was press, which is what WCW sorely needed.

Chapter V
Ted Turner's Surprising Play/Nitro

After the signing of Hogan and Savage, WCW coasted along steadily. It still wasn't attracting too much attention because it was purely syndicated and nothing else. It ran pay-per-views but had nothing special on TBS, other than their Saturday show. To make matters worse, the hype of Hogan's signing with the company was slumping fast.

While the *Saturday Night* show was a good timeslot to keep the ratings moderate, it still wasn't attracting the numbers of *Raw* because Saturday ratings don't tend to reach the levels of regular weeknight prime-time ratings.

With things looking to be turning around for WCW slowly but steadily, Bischoff wanted to keep things growing. Bischoff's initial idea for WCW going into 1995 was to sign a deal with an up-and-coming network known as Star TV, which was based in China. Star TV was becoming big quickly and buying out networks throughout Asia and part of Europe.

He saw this as a great way to grow WCW's global market, which was something that WCW always lacked when compared to the WWF. While a fine idea, he would need to pitch it in front of Turner in order for the plan to go through. He then made a call to Scott

Sassa, who was the President of Turner Entertainment Group at the time. Sassa, while not a huge wrestling fan, liked having it on TBS as it was keeping TBS afloat. He agreed with Bischoff's pitch and scheduled a meeting between himself, Bischoff and Turner.

The meeting, needless to say, didn't go as planned. Bischoff apparently only got partially into his pitch when Turner hit him with the infamous question, "What do we have to do to compete with Vince?"

Bischoff, out of sheer desperation, came up with an answer that he thought Turner would say no to because he wanted the Star TV deal. This answer wound up being to give him a prime time television slot.

A lot of people seem to wonder why Bischoff expected Turner to say no to this. It was actually the safest thing Bischoff could have said, at least from a business logic standpoint because the wrestling industry already had a prime time show and that was WWF *Raw*. With *Raw* already eating up 100% of the market in its timeslot, it would be insanely difficult, and some might have viewed it as impossible, to get any of its audience to jump ship and watch another program. In a way, Bischoff saw the idea as company suicide if they went for the prime time slot and a way for Turner to listen to the rest of his pitch.

Naturally, after saying this Turner looked over at Scott Sassa and told him to give Bischoff an hour on Monday nights on their flagship network, TNT.

This was a nightmare call for Bischoff and Sassa, Sassa in particular because he did not want wrestling on TNT. TNT was viewed across the board at Turner Broadcasting as Sassa's baby. He had made the network virtually his way and wrestling was not in his vision of the network.

Sassa did everything he could to stall Turner's decision during the meeting but there was no stopping it. Once Turner gave the orders for WCW to have a Monday night show, it was a done deal.

Bischoff, while initially surprised by Turner's answers, complied with the request without the slightest bit of hesitation. However, he knew that he would have to do his best to differ WCW's Monday night product from WWF's product. The first thing that was decided was to make it live.

As noted earlier, *Raw* was also live when it first started as well. Since WWF was a private company, it was a financial strain on the company to keep the show live. With WCW, this was not a problem. With Turner so confident on creating the show for Monday nights and his desire to compete with

McMahon, the budget was nothing to worry about with Bischoff.

Many factors had to be taken into account for the first show, which would be called *Monday Night Nitro*. The first would be the night the show would make its debut, which was selected to be September 4, 1995. A lot of people outside of the industry never saw the genius in Bischoff's choosing of this date. One of the problems with WWF's contract with the USA Network at that time was that they didn't have priority over special events on the network, which was a big hindrance to them as the battle was at its most cutthroat.

WCW was obviously very knowledgeable about this fact, so they decided to debut on a date when *Raw* would be pre-empted, this time by *U.S. Open Tennis*. So in order to garner the largest audience they possibly could for their debut, they chose a night where WWF would not be direct competition.

This was a very smart move on the part of Bischoff because it gave them a clean platform to put their show on. They would have had a much harder time getting people to see them had *Raw* been on the air. With them debuting when *Raw* was not on, they had a chance to keep a certain portion of the audience from watching Raw the following week.

The second factor was the location of the

debut. WCW was not in the condition to try and debut this show in a large arena and it would seem too much like their Saturday show if they kept it at the Disney/MGM Studio.

So instead of hosting it in some sort of sporting event venue, they hosted it at the Mall of America in Bloomington, Minnesota. While the event could only host *maybe* a few thousand people, it was a great venue from a presentation standpoint. Not only would there be seating surrounding the ring on the main floor, but there would be hundreds of people standing on the multiple floors above the ring and hundreds more on the escalators. It was a great looking show.

From a visual point-of-view, WCW's debut episode of *Nitro* was the best-looking show WCW had put on in years. The Mall of America looked awesome on television and made a good first impression of WCW on TNT.

One of the more remembered moments on the opening episode of *Nitro* was the return of Lex Luger to WCW.

Lex Luger's contract with the WWF had literally expired the night before *Nitro*. Luger had actually performed at a house show for the WWF on the last night of his contract.

Luger's reintroduction to WCW was a long road within itself. He had a nasty reputation for being unprofessional in his role with WCW during his previous tenure there. The only person that has gone on record of this, other than Bischoff, has been Sting, stating that there was a bit of unprofessionalism from him when Sting was on the rise and Luger was still struggling in his role.

Let's make one thing perfectly clear; Luger was never a great wrestler. He was someone who was brought in to both WCW and the WWF due to his look and nothing else, similar to Hogan. In fact, Luger was brought into the WWF to be Hogan's successor after the Ultimate Warrior turned out to be an ultimate failure.

Apparently, Sting was not very resentful towards Luger as he would be the one to help Bischoff make the decision on bringing Luger back. Sting had been in talks with Luger and was well aware of his contract expiring. Sting relayed the message to Bischoff to see what he wanted to do.

Given Bischoff's poor impression of Luger during his previous tenure with the company, he would have rather kicked him out as soon as he stepped foot into any meeting with him. Instead of doing that, he gave Luger an offer that was more of a test to Luger's seriousness on returning and his professionalism.

Luger was the highest paid wrestler in the

WWF at the time and was making close to, if not in the seven-digit income range. Bischoff offered Luger a one-year contract worth a hundred thousand dollars to see how serious he was. If things went well, a more lucrative contract would be discussed after the first year.

Much to Bischoff's surprise, Luger signed the contract and was set to make his debut on the first episode of *Nitro*. I always thought this contract signing spoke to Luger's character and willingness to work with Bischoff, especially considering how much money he was giving up.

Being a fan and seeing Luger walk out on-screen on *Nitro* that night was definitely a shock and a metaphor for what Bischoff wanted to do with the show.

One of the things about Professional Wrestling that's tough is being unpredictable; this has especially been tough for the business in recent years due to the rise of the internet. With the internet already becoming a factor then, becoming live would be a good way to keep the internet writers at bay.

This was one of the reasons why Bischoff wanted to keep the signing of Luger as private as possible. Apparently, the whole signing took place in Sting's garage, unannounced to everybody.

The debut of *Nitro* opened to a 2.5 rating, which was a strong number for a wrestling show at the time, and a strong number by cable television standards. The ball then began rolling from there.

Chapter VI
Dirty Tactics & Bret Hart

Both shows traded victories over the next year from that point on. Bischoff strove for *Nitro* to be different from the very beginning. The big difference between Bischoff and McMahon was that Bischoff had a more unconventional approach to his product.

McMahon was very much stuck in his ways at that time. Whether or not it was a personal preference or fear of another scandal, he stuck to a very safe pathway and that was keeping his show fit for families and no one else.

Bischoff on the other hand strove for a bigger and older audience. He also strove to get a lot of WWF's viewers as well, and this meant pulling some very dirty tactics on his show.

Bischoff hadn't been in the business long enough to know or care about how competition in the wrestling world was handled. In the sense of tradition, you never brought up your opponent on television, because usually, you were just asking for viewers to turn to the other show.

He didn't see it this way, he saw it as a way to get people to turn away from the WWF and tune into his show, or remain on his show and not keep switching back and forth between *Raw* and *Nitro*, which is what so many fans did at the beginning.

One of his more popular moves was giving away the results of *Raw's* taped shows on his live *Nitro*. Some saw this as unethical but I don't see it that way. This was competition, and in the world of competition, unless someone comes up with rules, you fight without gloves. If you want to win, you have to do whatever it takes.

These were million dollar companies butting heads with each other, so it should not have been a surprise that someone played dirty.

The biggest and most defining moment of how serious this rivalry was, during its beginning phase, was when WWF Women's Champion, Alundra Blaze, went to WCW.

A lot of people, including some within the business, thought that this jump happened while Blaze, now under the name Madusa in WCW, was still under contract with the WWF. This was not the case.

Madusa was actually released from her contract after winning the Woman's Title. The release from WWF was due to McMahon wanting to disband their woman's division. The WWF was struggling financially at the time and couldn't afford the women wrestlers on their roster any longer. So, instead of writing some elaborate story to end it, they just ended it unannounced because the division had not been on television very long to warrant a closure.

Now because of this, it is believed that Madusa was allowed to keep the belt because the WWF had no more use for it. She was released from WWF in December of 1995 and signed quickly to WCW and made her debut on *Nitro* on December 8.

Wanting to further stir the pot in the rivalry between the two companies, Bischoff had Madusa bring WWF's belt onto *Nitro*. Madusa has gone on record in saying that she did not want to bring the belt on television but was sort of forced by Bischoff. He was the boss and she was a brand new employee to them, so she really can't be blamed for going through with it.

She appeared on camera in an interview and picked up the belt and a trash can, and then proceeded to drop the Woman's Championship in the can.

This stirred a huge ball of fire with the WWF, to the point where the WWF took legal action against WCW. I always found it funny that WWF took legal action because they were equally as guilty only a few years earlier when they had Ric Flair walk on camera with the

WCW Title.

Either way, it was a huge deal and Bischoff knew it would be blown up when it happened live on television.

Despite doing these controversial things, WCW's ratings were still going up and down because they were not necessarily stellar in their creative department. They were still pulling dumb rabbits out of their hats, which included a stupid monster truck match between The Giant (Paul Wight aka Big Show) and Hulk Hogan. This immediately ruined any credibility that rivalry could have had.

White was an incredibly athletic big man back then and to me, that one Monster Truck match ruined that entire rivalry. They eventually did do an in-ring match between the two of them but that was even ruined by Hogan playing his usual creative control role as he did not want White to win the championship cleanly and instead did some stupid storyline where he won the belt by disqualification.

That's not to say WWF was reaching creative highs either. By the time 1996 rolled along, WWF had hired on Vince Russo in an attempt to steadily change the product. Russo decided to retaliate against WCW's blows and created the *Billionaire Ted* skits, in which WWF poked fun of Ted Turner, Hulk Hogan,

Randy Savage, and Gene Okerlund. The skits poked fun of Hogan and Savage's age and sort of depicted Turner as a rich idiot.

To Russo's credit, the skits were funny, but they weren't really measuring up to the things that Bischoff was doing. Bischoff was giving away results and tossing a WWF Championship in the garbage, while WWF was creating silly skits.

Bischoff has gone on record that he found the skits harmless, and has stated that both he and Turner found them to be very funny. While they were silly, USA Network was less than thrilled to have a parody of Ted Turner on their network. In fear of retaliation from Turner, they ordered McMahon to end the skits, which he agreed to and ended at the beginning of *Wrestlemania XII*.

While the skits might not have gotten the reaction that WWF was looking for, they did have one bit of creative genius at the time in my opinion, and that was Goldust (Dustin Runnels).

One of the things that Russo wanted to do with the product was add more controversial and adult elements to the show. As stated earlier, the WWF's product was primarily a family show up until that point. Goldust was a character designed to be very bizarre, pushing a homoerotic button on television. The character would grope himself and make homosexual gestures to his opponents. He was a character with gold and black face paint and a one-piece gold costume. To add to the weirdness of the character, he was joined by his real-life wife, Terri Runnels (going under the character name Marlena) as his valet, making him more of a bisexual character.

I loved the character of Goldust, it was a nice departure from what they had been doing prior. It was strange at first because he was the only character of his type in the WWF and wasn't the type of character you expected from them, but that's what made that character special. It's what also made his character all the more necessary for WWF at the time.

While both companies were proving to be hit and miss at the start of 1996, to me, it leaned in WWF's favor, mainly because of Shawn Michaels and Bret Hart.

WWF had an awesome rivalry going on with them in 1996. Hart and Michaels had some of the best chemistry ever and it stemmed from the fact that neither truly liked the other. There was a respect between them but there wasn't a friendship and that played out on-screen and made the two worth watching.

The two were set to meet at *Wrestlemania XII* in an Iron Man match, which was an idea provided by wrestling legend Pat Patterson. It is a sixty-minute match where the wrestler with the most pinfalls in the sixty-minutes wins.

While not many fans realized it at the time, *Wrestlemania XII* was a crucial event for the WWF. It needed to be a success. I am a firm believer that if this event, let alone the main event, did not succeed, WWF would not have survived 1996 as well as they did. The WWF was already under financial pressure and failure could have been crippling.

Wrestlemania XII was also significant because Bret Hart's contract was reaching its end. This was big news to the WWF because Bret Hart was their biggest star at the time, both in the states and all around the world. Hart had and still has an amazing international following and was WWF's biggest draw in Canada and Europe.

Wrestlemania XII was a huge success for the WWF, Hart and Michael's match could not have come off any better and was voted match of the year. The Iron Match was planned out perfectly between the two of them and is one of my favorite matches.

WWF had all the momentum in the world coming off of this event and actually gained a lot of fan interest in the weeks after. However, there was a significant flaw, they were missing

Bret Hart at that time and Hart would be gone until October.

Hart elected to sit out the rest of his contract to explore new options, not only from the WWF but also WCW. This was a very important moment during this time because it helped build on a rumor that WCW was stealing talent from the WWF.

Bischoff has defended himself on this and I agree wholeheartedly with Bischoff. Despite what WWE or any other journalist associated with them might make you think, WCW never stole or raided any roster.

Bischoff was smart enough and had the resources to know when someone's contract was up with the WWF, it's no different than a GM of a sports team finding out about a free agent on the market. Bischoff was in his legal right to make an offer to Hart, as long as his contract was up or the dates specified on his potential WCW contract was after Hart's current WWF contract's expiration date.

Also, once Hart's contract was up, he was free to go wherever he wanted or could elect to retire at that point; he definitely had the financial support to do so. Hart, was not ready to leave the ring. Although he was already 39, he could still out wrestle anyone he faced in the ring.

However, unlike his future offer, Bischoff

was not desperate for Hart at the time. If he wanted anything at all to do with Hart, it was over his global presence. WCW was still trying to grow on the global market and Hart was a surefire wrestler to have for that reason. But if Hart turned down the offer, Bischoff wasn't going to lose any sleep.

Hart's initial negotiations with WCW seemed to only be for the reason of getting Vince McMahon to offer him the best deal he could. He has gone on record in saying that he had no intentions of leaving WWF for WCW.

Bischoff's offer was for a three-year, nine million dollar contract, which was the largest contract Hart had ever been offered. Hart looked at the offer and went to McMahon to see what his retaliation would be.

While McMahon could not financially do the same, he offered Hart an unprecedented twenty-year contract for one and a half million per year, which Hart accepted. The contract was and still is the largest contract, in terms of years, in wrestling history.

Hart's absence during this time happened during the worst period for the WWF. Shortly after *Wrestlemania XII*, WWF would lose two of their top stars, Scott Hall and Kevin Nash (known as Razor Ramon and Diesel, respectively) and they both would go into WCW.

WCW than ran a story with the both of them, introducing them as the Outsiders, where they were portrayed as wrestlers from the WWF and they were set to take over the show. The WWF part of the storyline would have to be taken off the storyline due to legal action from McMahon.

The storyline was the best-written story that WCW had done in years. It couldn't have started any better either. The whole thing started when Hall disrupted a *Nitro* broadcast by walking through the crowd and doing a classic promo in the ring. Nash would appear on the program a couple weeks later and everything rolled from there.

One of the big reasons why I think this storyline worked so well was because they were literally on WWF's program only weeks before appearing on WCW. Seeing them make their debut on WCW was sort of surreal.

Fan interest was rising for WCW because of these two being on their program and it was great for WCW. They would then announce the addition of a third man.

Chapter VII
Heel Hulk Hogan & the NWO

In order for the Outsider angle to pay off, WCW needed to score a home run with the third man. Ratings were already beginning to shift in WCW's favor by June of 1996, but *Bash at the Beach* on July 7 would need to be big in order for the angle to keep holding water.

For this to work, a strong babyface character would need to turn heel and join The Outsiders. Initially, Bischoff had approached Sting over the opportunity. Sting would have actually worked well because he was viewed as the main babyface of the company. He had been their main babyface character for several years at that point.

According to Bischoff, Sting was very hesitant on the idea. He eventually agreed but Sting was having a hard time picturing himself as a heel.

With things appearing to be planned for action at *Bash at the Beach*, Bischoff received a call from Hogan to meet him on the set of a movie that he was filming, a dreadful picture called *Santa with Muscles*. If you've never seen it, consider yourself lucky; it makes *Jingle all the Way* look like Shakespeare.

Bischoff met Hogan after the picture had

wrapped for the day and Hogan inquired over the third man in The Outsiders group. Wanting to keep Sting's turn a secret, he gave Hogan an uncertain answer. Hogan immediately suggested himself.

Bischoff has stated that he had gone to Hogan on a previous occasion to speak with him on turning heel, in which Hogan politely threw Bischoff out of his house. Hogan was viewed as a babyface through and through. He was the guy that showed up at charities, he was the lead endorser on kids taking their vitamins and saying their prayers, and had been a babyface for over a decade by that point. So needless to say, this was a shock for Bischoff to hear.

Bischoff made it clear to Hogan that he would need to turn heel in order for him to be the third man, in which Hogan replied that he was already there.

This was actually very true. Hogan had not been well-received in WCW since his arrival. While still portraying his babyface persona, more and more fans were going against his character as many longtime WCW fans viewed him as the poster-child for the WWF, and someone who didn't belong in WCW.

Once it was clear that Hogan was very serious in his decision, Bischoff knew he struck gold. While Sting would have been big, Hogan was universe big. Hogan turning heel would not only get fans attention but the attention of the media as well.

Bischoff wanted to keep everything secret, including keeping it secret from the locker room. He told Sting sometime before the event of the change of plans, which Sting reportedly took well as he would not have to turn heel.

Bash at the Beach went along without a single error. The main event was going to be The Outsiders and a mystery third partner facing Randy Savage, Sting, and Lex Luger. The mystery partner was not revealed during most of the match.

As the match was reaching its end, Hall had hit a low blow on Savage while the referee was distracted. Hogan then came down and appeared to be helping Savage, Luger, and Sting, but then hit Savage with his Leg Drop, revealing himself to be the third man.

All pandemonium ensued from there and I'm not talking about the in-ring action, I'm talking about from fans. Fans began throwing garbage in the ring and one fan even jumped the guardrail to get to Hogan but was subdued by security, Hall, and Nash.

Hogan then cut one of his greatest promos on why he turned heel and announcing the group as the New World Order of wrestling.

The entire thing was classic to watch on television. I could only imagine what it was like to be in that arena and watching it all in person. Hogan showed how professional he truly was at cutting promos because he was getting pelted with trash throughout the entire promo and didn't stop for anything. In fact, Mean Gean Okerlund, who was conducting the interview, was hit in the face by a soda can, which caused blood to trickle down his nose.

The NWO was a big deal and I think over time, it's kind of been forgotten about on how big it was. There weren't really many groups at the time. Wrestling groups had kind of faded away in the early 90s' and wrestling groups were more known to be one dimensional. They could either be just a babyface or heel group with no in-between and if they were heels, they couldn't be cool to the fans.

The NWO was a group that was sort of counter-culture to the way groups were done, they were portrayed as their own entity and not just a group that was part of the company. There was them and then there was WCW; they were never viewed as one and the same.

I think because they were viewed as their own thing, it slowly made them cool. They were initially reviled by fans but as Hogan's Hollywood character began to take shape and

Hall and Nash began to get into their own changes, the group steadily became cool to the fans.

Let's face it, Hogan's first two-years as Hollywood Hulk Hogan were amazing. He was doing his best promo work, and while his matches were still not technical marvels, his position as a heel allowed him to hide his limitations and actually made him appear better in the ring than he ever had been.

One thing about the NWO angle that was very interesting was that it exposed how much the audience was changing in wrestling and WCW announcers tried to hide this through their entire run. As I stated earlier, they were becoming cool to watch and were actually getting strong reactions from the audience, to where the response was very mixed between them and whichever babyface they were in the ring with.

This positive response led to a shift in the ratings that would remain in WCW's favor for nearly two years.

Chapter VIII
WWF Changes, Stone Cold Steve Austin, and the Curtain Call

While WCW's change in pace was very prominent, WWF was a bit slower in their lane but that doesn't mean that changes weren't happening. As I have stated earlier, they had introduced Goldust onto the roster, which was a huge departure for them.

But someone else was also introduced at the time and it was a character known as The Ringmaster, who was portrayed by Steve Austin (Steve Williams at the time). Austin had previously worked with WCW and had garnered success as a singles and tag team wrestler (The Hollywood Blondes with Brian Pillman as his partner). He had been injured during a match, where he tore his tricep off his elbow and was left out of action.

WCW and the then newly appointed Executive Producer Eric Bischoff tried to work with him while he was injured but Austin wasn't happy with WCW and became difficult to work with. This led to Bischoff firing Austin.

Austin would make a brief transition into a smaller organization called ECW (we'll discuss them later). While there, Austin really honed his interview and promo skills, especially since he couldn't wrestle much due to injury. Austin was then noticed by WWF superstar Bret Hart.

Hart has gone on record in saying that he saw Austin coming before anyone else and given their future history together, I wouldn't doubt it. Hart requested for McMahon to try and get Austin on their roster because he saw great potential in him. There is also a rumor that Kevin Nash also had a hand in Austin's hiring as well.

Austin agreed to sign on to the WWF and was brought in under The Ringmaster gimmick in late 1995 and was managed by wrestling legend Ted Debiase. I don't think I'm saying anything new when I say that The Ringmaster gimmick was one of the worst characters they could have given Austin.

Yes, Austin was a much faster and more polished wrestler at the time (before his neck injury) but by having someone else as his mouthpiece and a lame character name, there wasn't much growth for him under that marquee.

Austin saw the limitations on the wall under The Ringmaster and requested a change. After receiving a terrible list of names from the WWF, he would actually get his name from his wife at the time, and that name was Stone Cold Steve Austin.

Austin would soon enter into a minor

rivalry with Savio Vega, where a match would determine the future of Debiase as his manager. After losing the match, Debiase was forced to leave the WWF. In reality, Debiase left the company, choosing not to renew with the WWF, and choosing to go over to WCW.

Debiase leaving opened the door for Austin as a singles performer. He would open up more on the microphone and become a more vulgar and violent character than the WWF had seen up to that point. He would make the middle finger part of his promos, which was a USA Network censorship nightmare.

Things would really turn around for Austin's character on June 23, 1996, at the *King of the Ring*. The history behind that year's *King of the Ring* is very interesting, because as legendary of an event as it was, Austin's moment at *King of the Ring* almost didn't happen.

The WWF had different plans leading up to the event and it actually involved another up-and-comer at the time, and that was Hunter Hearst Helmsley (Paul Levesque aka Triple H). Triple H was another superstar that had come from WCW and sought a bright future with the WWF.

Triple H had all of the tools to be a huge superstar and was making the most out of a pretty lame character. He was portraying a blue-blood from Greenwich, Connecticut. He was a character that was very snobby and talked down to the audience. It wasn't a great character but Triple H made the character appealing and that showed how good he was. Because he was that good, McMahon saw gold with him and wanted him to be the winner of the *King of the Ring* that year.

Things obviously didn't transpire like this as one huge event would keep Triple H down. Just one month before the event, on May 19, 1996, Triple H, Shawn Michaels, Kevin Nash, and Scott Hall were all having matches at a Madison Square Garden house show.

This night would be the last night of both Nash and Hall's contracts with the WWF before they would head off to WCW. All four of them were and still are the closest of friends. Their friendship was known as the *Kliq* and they were not a very popular group with many other wrestlers backstage.

It was actually a well-kept secret that Nash and Hall were leaving, and fans were pretty much unaware that this would be their last matches with the company.

The house show at Madison Square Garden was big; it was WWF's first sold out house show at that facility in years, so they tried to make it as big as possible. But no match was bigger than the event that took place at the end of the night.

Instead of saying goodbye to each other backstage or at some bar after the fact, they all decided to say goodbye to each other in the ring. They hugged each other and showed off their friendship to everyone, even though their characters were enemies of each other. This became known as *The Curtain Call*. Back in those days, no one within the industry admitted that wrestling was scripted. WWF didn't do it, nor did WCW.

By all four of them showing off their friendship in front of thousands of people, it instantly gave all of that away. Also, much to WWF's chagrin, someone in the audience filmed the entire thing.

McMahon has gone on record that he allowed this to transpire since it was a house show and figured no one would notice or care afterward. However, the backstage backlash from many veteran wrestlers forced McMahon to step up and punish someone for it.

Shawn Michaels was champion at the time and was virtually untouchable. Kevin Nash and Scott Hall were leaving, so they couldn't be held accountable. The only one left was Triple H. As part of Triple H's punishment, he was no longer a superstar on the rise and wouldn't be for another year. He would be placed on the lowest point of the card and would be taken out of any possible title picture. Last but not least, he would not win the *King of the Ring*.

Since Triple H would not be winning, McMahon had to think fast and choose a wrestler who could carry the ball and run with it and Steve Austin was that guy.

Interestingly enough, Austin replacing Triple H resulted in one of the most underrated matches in Austin's career and that was the semi-final match in the tournament with Marc Mero. Mero at the time was portraying a higher flying wrestler, which he would change to a boxing gimmick a year later.

Austin was at the peak of his wrestling abilities in 1996 in my opinion, and he proved how well he could perform when he faced Mero. It's one of those matches that seems to have faded away from a lot of memories over time but is definitely worth checking out.

Because Austin was a last minute replacement, there wasn't a lot the creative team could think of to help Austin along for when he won, so Austin would have to come up with a lot of his performance at *King of the Ring* on his own.

Austin's speech has remained one of the most memorable in wrestling history and really only lasted for a few minutes. It's actually my second favorite in wrestling history, my first being Jake Roberts' promo on Ted Debiase at *Wrestlemania VI*. Ironically, Roberts would be Austin's opponent in the finals of the tournament and it would be Roberts that would inspire the speech.

Roberts was portraying a more religious character at the time and Austin used that for motivation for his speech.

Austin's ascension in the ranks would continue over the next few months. A lot of people tend to wonder why WWF didn't push him a lot sooner and it was a little more obvious to see then than it is now. Austin's character was still very much in its beginning phases. Fans didn't quite know what to think of him, and a lot of the trademark features for the character had yet to come to fruition at that time.

As the character took shape and his promos began to evolve into the promos that the character became known for, it began to appeal to the audience. Austin's character was supposed to be a heel through and through but about a month after his win at *King of the Ring*, the crowd began to shift slightly. More and more people began to cheer for him and WWF tried to hide this as best as they could because they wanted to keep him in that heel position because Austin was very good in that role.

The first obvious crowd that showed that Austin's popularity was rising was at the In Your House pay-per-view, *Buried Alive* in Indianapolis. Austin faced the originally planned winner of the *King of the Ring*, Triple H. It was meant to be a heel versus heel match but Austin got a noticeably loud pop from the crowd and the announcers did their best to hide it. That was the first time that Austin's rising popularity was noticeable.

Unfortunately, despite an obviously rising star in Austin and a fair amount of good creative work coming out of the WWF, there wasn't any competing with WCW at the time. By June of that year, WCW was starting to hit hard and had taken a lead in the ratings that would almost seem permanent.

Chapter IX
Sting Reinvented and the Cruiserweight Division

With the introduction of The Outsiders, which would eventually lead to the NWO, WCW became the show to watch. The entire NWO storyline was fascinating. But while fascinating with the audience, there wasn't a lot of fascination with some of the others in the locker room.

Because the NWO was so important and so cool, they were written to beat up and humiliate a lot of the top babyfaces in the company, which didn't sit well with a lot of wrestlers because they weren't allowed to retaliate most of the time.

However, there was one wrestler that took this as an opportunity and that was Sting. For most of his career, much like Hogan, he was the big babyface. He was the character that could do no wrong.

With the audience around the entire landscape of wrestling changing, Sting knew he would have to change. While he could still remain the babyface, he couldn't be the clean-cut babyface anymore. He could no longer do the flattop haircut and the colorful face paints anymore.

On September 16, 1996, Sting came down

to the ring unannounced, with no music and no attempt to pump up the crowd over his entrance. The entire promo was well thought out with Sting declaring himself a free agent and also facing away from the camera the entire time he did the promo, which made it very effective to the audience at home. He would then walk out on the show. He would disappear for a month after that.

There was actually a lot of thought that went into the evolution of Sting's character. It was pretty much known from the start of this process that Sting was going to be a darker character than the character he had been portraying. The main question was, how dark and what would the character now look like?

Surprisingly, it would be Scott Hall that would come up with the new look for the character. Hall was obviously a fan of *The Crow*, which is a classic film among comic book films. The new look for Sting's character would borrow heavily from *The Crow*.

He would grow his hair out and his colorful face paint was replaced with a near all-white paint. Initially, the new paint on his face was shaped in the same manner as his original face paint. He also had black lines going vertically over his eyes.

Sting was one of my favorite wrestlers growing up and I was nine when Sting changed his character. It was really eerie seeing him walk down the aisle with the new look and it still has a profound effect now, especially when you watch his career in order.

Initially, the new look was looked at by fans as a possible tease for his heel turn and him joining the NWO. This would turn out not to be as Sting would walk away from the NWO during his debut in the white makeup.

He would then become a much more brooding character, hiding out in the rafters of the arenas and watching down on the action below. It was creepy but addicting to see on television and made for some classic moments. It's stuff like this that makes it easy to see why WCW became so dominant.

Sting would then enter a long-running feud with Hogan that would span over a year.

It wasn't just this that brought in the ratings for WCW. Bischoff knew that he couldn't just rely on the big, larger than life characters of the past. He would need a younger, smaller, and more athletic division to make up his mid-card matches. He would then recruit wrestlers for his Cruiserweight division, which consisted of wrestlers such as, Chris Jericho, Chris Benoit, Eddie Guerrero, Rey Mysterio Jr., Saturn, Dean Malenko, and more.

These were wrestlers that were either high

flyers, or unbelievable technical wrestlers. There were hardly any bad matches with these guys. These were wrestlers that knew how to deliver and knew how to tell a story in the ring. In fact, the mid-card matches with this division, more often than not, became more entertaining than that of the main event guys.

A lot of these wrestlers were brought in from outside sources, Mexico, Japan, or ECW.

With that said, this does bring up one of the main criticisms that slammed WCW from the moment Bischoff entered into WCW to the last day of the company's existence and that was Bischoff buying talent from elsewhere and not creating his own stars from scratch.

For WCW, it can be argued that in 1995 they didn't have enough of a roster to build the company from scratch; they needed the established big names and mid-card wrestlers to even have any remote chance to survive. Yes, this would eventually be a contributing factor to their demise, which we'll touch on later, but there wouldn't have been a chance for survival from the start if they hadn't made the decision to sign them.

For the mid-card roster, these were wrestlers that were already established in other territories, outside of WCW, especially in Canada, Mexico, and Japan. So, in some ways, they were big stars in their own right, just not in the states.

It was for this reason that made signing them pure genius on the part of Bischoff. These were wrestlers that could deliver quality matches and attract an audience that might have been very foreign to the company, while also providing a style of wrestling to the established WCW fan base that had yet to be seen.

WCW's mid-card lineup was by far the best out of the two companies from 95-98. They had tremendous depth and a style of wrestling that was unmatched. Guys like Benoit, Malenko, Mysterio, and more could do no wrong in that ring.

On the WWF's side of things, they had depth in their mid-card as well. As I stated, guys like Stone Cold and Triple H were slowly moving up the ranks, but there wasn't enough of a mid-card that compared to WCW, in my opinion.

If I had to nitpick on anything wrong with WCW's mid-card, it was their storylines. WCW seemed to build the mid-card primarily for matches rather than storytelling, unlike their heavyweight division, which was all story with very little wrestling.

I feel WCW missed a big chance here because they could have experienced the best of both worlds with the Cruiserweight division by giving them more complex storylines and having incredible matches. For instance, guys like Jericho, Benoit and Guerrero were great storytellers, and while that would be proven later on in their careers, it should have been exploited then. That alone would have added more depth their matches and made them more fun to watch than they already were.

Chapter X
ECW

Okay, I've kept from talking about it up to this point, but seeing how we've approached the mid-90s', I will talk about ECW, *Extreme Championship Wrestling*. I'll go over them in the next few chapters but keep it short and sweet. ECW, while smaller, did play a role in the feud between WCW and WWF. ECW was a smaller, almost regional-like promotion based out of Philadelphia. Originally known as Tri-State Wrestling, it was purchased by Todd Gordon in 1992 and renamed *Eastern Championship Wrestling*.

At the time, ECW was part of the rapidly declining NWA. By 1992, its largest promotion, WCW, had already cut ties with it after Ted Turner had bought it in 1988, so the NWA was struggling to remain relevant in the world of Professional Wrestling.

Todd Gordon saw the writing on the wall for the NWA and wanted to slowly change ECW into something different from the rest of the world of wrestling. These changes conflicted with their lead booker at the time, Eddie Gilbert. Gilbert would leave the company after many conflicts with Gordon.

This would lead to the signing of Paul Heyman in September of 1993. Heyman had previously worked at WCW as an on-screen manager, most notably managing Steve Austin during the start of his career.

From a creative standpoint, Heyman is probably the best man for any booking job in wrestling. Heyman has a very good creative mind and knows how to create a wrestling show.

Gordon and Heyman were a pair that the NWA didn't particularly care for but they were looking to build some steam for the company and with ECW generating more traction and being one of the very few regional promotions left that could succeed, they turned to ECW for a championship tournament for the NWA Championship.

The tournament was the brainchild of Jim Crockett, and he pitched the tournament idea to Gordon, who accepted the idea. However, NWA President Dennis Coralluzzo didn't trust Crockett, nor did he trust Gordon or Heyman. He viewed Crockett's idea as a way to monopolize the title, meaning that the title would be under ECW only and no longer under the NWA.

For safety, Coralluzzo oversaw the entire tournament. Shane Douglas was written to win the title. Douglas was a wrestler who was rejected from going anywhere else but ECW due to his rumored work ethic but Gordon and Heyman were two men who believed in him and he was with ECW for the long haul.

While Douglas was written to win, Gordon didn't want the NWA title in ECW. One of the reasons Coralluzzo didn't trust ECW was because Gordon had already expressed interest in separating ECW from the NWA, and trying to compete on a more mainstream level.

The tournament seemed to go along just fine for Coralluzzo up until the very end of it when Douglas won. Douglas held the belt in his hands and seemed to be giving a heartfelt speech, but then threw the belt on the ground and picked up the newly formed ECW Championship. At that very moment, ECW established itself as its own entity, breaking all ties with the NWA.

The split between the two companies wasn't without its arguments as Coralluzzo fought his heart out to get Douglas stripped of both the ECW title and the NWA title but Gordon stood his ground and fought for Douglas and would make the announcement of ECW's split public shortly after the tournament and would rename the company, Extreme Championship Wrestling.

ECW for a majority of the 90s' was broadcast primarily on public access channels and more regional networks such as MSG or Sports Channel Philadelphia. They would develop a more violent and crude style of wrestling than that of the WWF and WCW. Heyman was a huge factor in the development of the ECW brand and what it would represent and promote on-screen.

Also, because the company was not nationally known, they could get away with things that neither McMahon nor Bischoff could, which resulted in a product that was far different from theirs. However, this did bring on problems for the company that was very noticeable early on. It's more violent style (which wrestling would dub the *Hardcore* style) did make them unappealing to more well-known networks.

ECW had a hell of a time getting out of the public access channels for many years. While keeping the company in its hardcore format, they tried to change things up a bit and add more pure wrestling matches. They signed many of the wrestlers in 1994 that would take up WCW's Cruiserweight division later on. Wrestlers like Chris Benoit, Chris Jericho, Dean Malenko, and Eddie Guerrero.

This did make ECW very different from WWF and WCW from a wrestling standpoint, as the technical and high flying styles of wrestling were not quite as big in the states as they were in other countries.

Their tenure in ECW was very short-lived

as WCW would start to acquire more talent for *Nitro* in 1995, and would turn to ECW for much of their talent. Now there have been rumors that Todd Gordon was going behind Heyman's back and selling talent to WCW, which led to Gordon's release from ECW. Before any of this had happened, earlier in that very same year, Gordon had sold ECW to Heyman as ECW's expansion was surpassing the budget he had planned, making him unable to handle the company.

Some have stated that the budget side of the story was a flat-out lie on Gordon's part and only a way to make his actions less noticeable as he would no longer be under the close eye of Heyman on a business level.

Others have stated that the talent being sent to WCW was more of a personal decision from the wrestlers, rather than Heyman's or Gordon's. Bischoff has been the one to really defend that side of the story. Bischoff's side of the story has been that he reached out to the talent and made the offer with no say from anyone at ECW.

This might be unpopular for me to say, but I agree with Bischoff. Bischoff, from a legal standpoint, didn't need the say from anybody on getting any of the talent from ECW, other than the agreement of the talent themselves. ECW was not a company in a position to contract anybody to their roster, and a majority of them were not being paid much, if any money at all as it was a smaller promotion with no sponsorship whatsoever.

A lot of the talent seemed to leave both for personal and professional reasons, because why stay with a company for life if you can't afford to live your life working there.

Most of 95-96 saw ECW just trying to establish itself. Heyman, while a great creative mind, didn't have the business mind to work with ECW as it continued to grow, so he got his family involved as investors for the company and worked with various partners to help him with the business side of it.

Chapter XI
ECW & WWF, Mass Transit, Barely Legal

1995 also marked a time when WWF became very aware of ECW. During the *King of the Ring* in ECW's hometown of Philadelphia that year, the crowd began randomly chanting "ECW" throughout the arena. Vince McMahon, who was the lead television commentator at the time, merely didn't acknowledge the chants and not much seemed to be made out of it within the company.

This apparently wasn't the case as the WWF would return to Philadelphia in 1996 for one of their In Your House pay-per-view's, *Mind Games*. McMahon and Heyman had been corresponding for some time up until the pay-per-view and McMahon saw it as a good cross-promotional opportunity. So, during the match between Savio Vega and Bradshaw, Tommy Dreamer, The Sandman and Paul Heyman were all sitting in the front row during the match.

Towards the tail end of the match, Sandman stood up and spit beer in Vega's face. In order to keep things secret between the two companies and make it look real, security in the building had no idea the incident was going to occur, making for one of the most random but memorable moments for

ECW at the time.

After that, WWF didn't really acknowledge ECW much on-screen. However, the behind-the-scenes proceedings between the two companies were far different. McMahon saw great talent in ECW but didn't want to rob ECW of all their talent. He put ECW on the WWF's payroll to keep bringing in talent from ECW but also sending development talent to ECW.

ECW being on WWF's payroll has generated a lot of rumors of Heyman being on the WWF's payroll, which led to the negative rumor of him getting paid and not paying his own talent. Both Heyman and McMahon have opposed this rumor. Heyman has stated the reason for ECW being on the payroll of the WWF was over Too Cold Scorpio. One of the very view sponsors that ECW had at the time was over Scorpio's music; ECW received a grand per week to play his entrance music.

With Scorpio leaving for the WWF, this grand per week would go away as well. McMahon compensated for the loss by paying ECW a grand per week. On top of that Heyman has said that any financial compensation that ECW received was never placed in his own pocket and only used for ECW.

As much as I like Heyman as a creative

mind, I have been inclined to call bullshit on this story. True, I don't know the facts of it and I don't know what was said behind closed doors, but given the relationship between the two companies, particularly the business relationship that McMahon and Heyman built, and an agreement that Heyman would have a job should ECW fold, it does make it tough to believe that Heyman wasn't personally compensated.

Don't get me wrong, I don't say this to demean Heyman in any way or question his loyalty to the company because there was no one more loyal to ECW than Paul Heyman. Heyman believed in the product and the progress it would make, no matter how long it took to make it.

But by late 1996, the slow progression needed to work a little more quickly for ECW. While their fan base was growing, their finances weren't. They needed to expand further out of the realm of local television. In order to do that, the next step for them would be pay-per-view. Pay-per-view was a valuable asset to the world of Professional Wrestling. I dare say it was more important to wrestling than any other business on the face of the earth.

ECW though, unlike the WWF and WCW, had a lot of trouble finding a provider. ECW's violent, sexual, and crude content didn't sit well with providers. This was long before the age of UFC on cable television, so providers were much sterner on what was broadcast.

After many tries, Heyman landed a deal with Request TV, for March 30th, under the normal time slot of 7 P.M. Heyman and the rest of the locker room could not have been happier as it was their chance to show the world what they were made of.

After securing the deal, ECW continued to tour the east coast and ran into trouble on November 23, 1996. They were hosting a show in Revere, Massachusetts and one of the matches was with D-Von Dudley and Axl Rotten facing New Jack and Mustafa Saed. Axl Rotten didn't make it to the show that night due to what was said to be a family emergency. Rotten would confirm that it was due to Heyman not buying him a plane ticket to Boston for the show.

In order to keep the match as scheduled, they needed to find a replacement. Since it was such short notice, Heyman chose a guy he had talked to named Eric Kulas, going under the gimmick Mass Transit. He had stated that he was 23 years of age and was trained by the legendary Killer Kowalski.

The match was planned with New Jack set to blade Kulas in the ring. For those unfamiliar with this term, blading means cutting one's self with a blade or another wrestler doing it for them to make them start bleeding in the match. This is usually done with a small razor blade but sometimes it can vary.

New Jack would blade him with a surgical scalpel and severed two arteries in Kulas' forehead. Kulas screamed in pain, but due to the blood loss had passed out shortly after. New Jack and Saed continued to work on Kulas even after the match, prompting Kulas' father to yell for the bell and admit his real age.

Request TV would catch wind of the incident and would cancel ECW's pay-per-view on Christmas Eve. Heyman pleaded like a mad man to get the event back on schedule and once he was able to convince Request TV that he was misled by Kulas, the event was placed back on schedule. However, the provision for it being placed back on the schedule would be to move it to a 9 P.M. timeslot, which was one of the lowest viewed timeslots on pay-per-view, but for ECW, it was either take it or leave it. The pay-per-view would fittingly be called *Barely Legal*.

The announcement of the pay-per-view hit the WWF and McMahon would contact Heyman to help promote the event. ECW would be part of WWF *Raw* on February 24, 1997. *Raw* would return to the Manhattan Center for this show as it would fit in better with ECW. The entire storyline was that ECW was invading *Raw*. Wrestlers from ECW would either interfere or they would actually have matches.

There would also be an on-screen rivalry between Jerry Lawler and ECW. Lawler had off-screen personal problems with ECW and has been vocal on McMahon's decision to involve them in their program, but Lawler, being a professional, did everything he was instructed to do without argument.

The rivalry was pretty cool with Lawler actually making a surprise appearance on ECW's syndicated show.

It was rather interesting to see ECW on *Raw* and for some reason, it didn't come off as surprising. *Raw* was at its lowest point of the ratings war and McMahon obviously saw this as an opportunity to probably turn the tide and change the product around.

There had already been some slight changes going on in the WWF, most of which we will get to later, but long story short, ECW fit the direction that McMahon wanted to take the company in.

ECW also had a valuable asset in their company that would play a huge role in *Barely*

Legal's success and that was Terry Funk. Funk was already a living legend by 1997and was still going strong despite being in his 50's. Funk's name brought much-needed recognition to the company, which it was lacking before he arrived.

Funk saw an enormous amount of potential in ECW and was a company that he vowed to get off the ground. Heyman and Funk were like mad scientists because they knew the formula that the event needed to make a success out of it.

Barely Legal is one of the best first pay-per-view's I've ever seen from a wrestling company. ECW needed to hit a home run and they did. The event was ECW's chance to make their statement on a national level and they couldn't have done any better. While their company put on great events after this, *Barely Legal* I think shines as their best.

Barely Legal drew a .25 buyrate for ECW, which is equivalent to about one thousand buys. While it was nowhere near what WWF and WCW were drawing for their pay-per-view events, it was a great debut for a company that mainly broadcast on the east coast. They were off to the races from there.

Chapter XII
TNN and Bankruptcy

Like most races, the racer usually slows down after a while and unfortunately ECW's speed couldn't rely on pay-per-views alone. Despite a string of successful pay-per-views from 97-99, their finances continued to decline.

This was not so much the fault of ECW as it was the fault of the time-period for wrestling. Wrestling was so far into the mainstream that big named wrestlers were now requiring outlandish payrolls. Paul Heyman described it best as the industry being an "inflated bubble that had to burst". ECW lost a bunch of talent to the WWF and WCW during this time but still had a stellar group of wrestlers in Tazz, The Dudley Boyz, Sandman, Shane Douglas, Tommy Dreamer, and of course Rob Van Dam. So it wasn't like they didn't have a good roster.

Much like the problem that Total Nonstop Action (TNA) faced just a few years ago, ECW was a company that needed to expand further than just pay-per-view. Heyman went on a search for a network for the company to apply its trade.

There was a slight problem, and that was despite wrestling being the thing to watch in

1999, there were still networks that were very apprehensive to have it on their schedules due to the content and with ECW being the most adult of the three companies, it didn't put things in their favor.

However, ECW did appear to strike gold in the middle of the year, and that would be with a rookie network known as *The Nashville Network* (it would be renamed *The National Network* and is currently named *Spike TV*). TNN was a network looking to expand its content. They had finally secured deals with most cable companies in the country and needed to broaden their content beyond what they were typically known for (monster trucks, motocross, etc...).

TNN needed to know what shows would and wouldn't work. ECW was used as the guinea pig to see if wrestling would attract a new audience and be accepted by their current audience.

Paul Heyman signed a three-year contract with TNN and it was probably one of the worst deals ever devised. TNN had, and still has as *Spike TV*, one of the worst reputations in cable television when it comes to contracts with television shows.

TNN was very much a pencil-pushing company and saved every dime they could, even if it meant their show going into financial ruin. Heyman signed a deal where ECW had no commercial time and would have to provide the budget for their weekly show.

For ECW, the budget was everything to the deal. ECW didn't have a budget to run on to be on television. They hardly even had a budget once expenses were paid for the company.

To make matters worse, they were going on a network that was very green when it came to broadcasting content that was in their league. This meant a lot of frightened executives at TNN. The network was less than willing to let ECW get away with the things that they had gotten away with on public access and local networks.

Heyman even received advice from McMahon that he would have to change the product in order to appeal to a national audience. Heyman stood steadfast when it came to the programming his show presented and did everything he could to defy the network.

One of the common misconceptions about ECW's relationship with TNN was that TNN was the source of all the problems the two organizations had with each other, which couldn't have been any further from the truth.

I agree, TNN's deal was not the best in the industry but it wasn't their fault that Heyman signed it without reading further into it or consulting a lawyer. Also, Heyman's constant defiance of the network wasn't going to win any executives over either. A great example of this was their very first episode on TNN. ECW gave their written agreement to broadcast brand new wrestling on the network. Instead, because Heyman wasn't impressed with their first shows taping, they aired older matches and promos from various pay-per-views. Had TNN been in the position that they are in now, they probably would have torn their contract in front of Heyman then.

I firmly believe that these actions are what led to TNN's ultimate dislike of ECW. I also believe that if ECW had complied with the rules set for them from the start, TNN would have kept them on long-term, instead of wanting to get rid of them as quickly as they did.

TNN's dislike for ECW (particularly Heyman) was so big that they refused to acknowledge ECW's show as their top program. ECW, to their credit, was the highest rated show that the network had ever had up to that point, consistently in the one to two million viewer range for their entire run. TNN refused to acknowledge this and instead chose to try and get as much attention to their show, *Roller Jam*, which was acquired around the same time as ECW.

ECW and *Roller Jam* were TNN's highest rated two-hour block but neither were getting the numbers the network needed to compete, despite ECW's high numbers. Because wrestling was proving to be a popular choice for the network, they reached out to WWF when word got out that WWF's contract with USA Network was expiring in September of 2000. McMahon was already expressing interest in switching networks so that *Raw* could be on a network where their show would no longer be pre-empted every other month due to other events. TNN offered McMahon over twenty-eight million dollars to switch networks, which was accepted.

Word of the deal spread rapidly, especially to Heyman. Heyman was so infuriated of the news that he went on the air during one of the tapings and berated the network on the show. TNN would end up muting the whole thing and putting a scroll on the bottom, stating how insane Paul Heyman was.

WWF made its debut on TNN on September 25, 2000. There were many rumors floating that both WWF and ECW would co-exist on TNN. This rumor was created because of the known relationship between ECW and WWF, and the fact that *Raw* was on Monday's and ECW was on Friday. This would not be the case as TNN would cancel ECW only two weeks into WWF's run with the network.

ECW was in a financial state where they couldn't survive without a network. Heyman actually looked into a deal with Fox Sports Network. Fox was very interested in ECW and wanted to do an hour long show on Saturday's. According to Heyman, because of the financial offer in the contract, he couldn't accept.

Heyman did not reveal the Fox deal until over a decade after the company closed its doors. It was this deal that made Heyman seem like the fool. Heyman has said countless times that if the company had gotten onto another network, the company would have survived. He then reveals that he had this offer and refused it.

Granted, we'll never know the rules and regulations of the offer but the fact that ECW was on pins and needles at the time and needed a network deal to stay in business, it didn't make any sense on why the deal was refused. I honestly think that if this was the case, Heyman is the biggest fool on the planet.

I know me saying that is not going to be popular because Heyman is so loved by many fans, but it can't be denied that Heyman is a bad businessman. His own wrestlers have stated how bad of a businessman he was and

I think that deal alone proves that.

With the company in peril and seemingly no way out, Heyman just would stop showing up to the shows, appearing to give up. This would leave the job of creative to ECW veteran Tommy Dreamer, but the position would only last a few weeks as Heyman would file bankruptcy.

ECW's announcement of bankruptcy was known to absolutely nobody until Heyman showed up on *Raw* on March 10, 2001. Heyman would replace Jerry Lawler as the second lead announcer on *Raw* after Lawler had a falling out with McMahon. It would be Jim Ross and himself on the broadcast team for the majority of 2001.

So, to really sum up ECW, it was a company that was best described by Paul Heyman, a company that was too big to be small and too small to be big. Out of the three companies, they were definitely the most ambitious but just didn't have the horsepower of their larger competitors. ECW strove to be unique and be something that the WWF and WCW weren't. In the end, they just didn't have the resources of those companies, nor the correct businessman guiding the ship to get it to the level that it deserved to be at.

Chapter XIII
Bret Hart Returns, a Changing Attitude, and the Montreal Screwjob

As stated earlier, Bret Hart had taken a hiatus from wrestling after *Wrestlemania XII* to explore his future in the business. He explored options from both the WWF and WCW, choosing to take an unprecedented twenty-year contract with the WWF for one and a half million dollars a year.

Hart would take eight months off before returning on *Raw* and announcing his decision to stay with the WWF live on television. He would immediately enter into a rivalry with up-and-comer Stone Cold Steve Austin, as the two would share some of the greatest matches of both of their careers.

Hart's return to television was great when it happened and fans initially responded very well to his return as it had been so long since he had been on television. However, the responses for him in the weeks afterward were becoming more and more different.

Hart's fan reactions were steadily changing leading up to *Wrestlemania XII* but WWF didn't quite acknowledge it then. By November of 1996, the crowds started to pull away a little more. While he was still receiving very loud reactions, they weren't nearly as strong as they had been years prior.

As the rivalry evolved with Steve Austin, it was becoming more and more noticeable that Austin's popularity was steadily growing and Hart and Austin's first match at *Survivor Series* that year would be the first time that it would be acknowledged on television by the announcers as Austin's crowd response at Madison Square Garden was very vocal.

Austin was red hot leading up to the latter half of 1996, constantly challenging Hart throughout the year while Hart was on hiatus. He was the perfect match for Hart when it came to being a character that could really contrast with Hart's and that contrasting image started to grow with the fans.

McMahon took a strong notice of this change and decided to steadily change Hart's character leading into 1997. Hart began running more and more promos where he denounced the WWF and how he felt he had been screwed upon his return to the company.

Hart's gradual journey to turn heel was initially not well-received by Hart himself. Much like Hogan, Hart was brought up as a character that was a good guy through and through. However, Hart's case was a little different than Hogan's because his international presence was one of the things that eclipsed Hogan and it was one of the factors that made the decision tough.

For any strong babyface in wrestling, it's always tough to change your image, because with good guy images like Hart and Hogan, you not only play this role in wrestling but also to the general public and that is how the public perceives you. It's especially difficult when the brunt of your fan base is children because they take it more seriously than anybody.

While the decision was slow, Hart agreed to take on the heel role as it was becoming more apparent that most fans were becoming bored with his character.

Hart's dissension into the heel role is one of my all-time favorites. WWF wanted to play it as subtly as possible without making it feel forced. The slow process literally started shortly after his return, all the way until *Wrestlemania 13*.

As the months went on, Hart's character continued to change. It was going from confident good guy to a whining bad guy.

However, the full heel turn was initially supposed to be different leading into *Wrestlemania*. Hart's rivalry with Steve Austin was originally supposed to end in late 1996 after the *Survivor Series* but things had to be rewritten very quickly in February of 1997, only one month before *Wrestlemania 13*.

Shawn Michaels had recaptured the WWF Championship at the *Royal Rumble* that year. The initial plan for *Wrestlemania* was to have the highly demanded rematch between Hart and Michaels. This had been planned out many months before *Wrestlemania* and seemed like a done deal. Michael's however, would deliver his famous *I Lost my Smile* promo where he forfeited the belt and would supposedly leave due to a knee injury.

Many, including Hart, felt that Michaels purposely forfeited the title so that he wouldn't have to wrestle Hart again and lose the belt. It's tough to say whether Hart was correct in his suspicions or Michaels was telling the truth.

On one hand, you have a very tense relationship between Hart and Michaels. They were two people who couldn't stand one another and both Hart and McMahon have stated that Michael's had openly admitted at one point before all of this that he would never lose to Hart.

But then there was Michaels, who wrestled a very aggressive, high-flying style that was constantly getting himself injured and would actually get him injured the following year. Michael's has stated in later interviews that he was being honest and did have surgery on his knee. It's a tough call; the story could go either way.

Because of the quick change, Hart and Austin continued their rivalry, which led to their submission match at *Wrestlemania*. Austin has gone on record that he had no idea of the submission match until it was announced on a taped edition of *Raw* that he saw from home because he was suffering from his first knee injury.

In many ways, Michael's injury was perfectly timed for both Hart and Austin, because the submission match would become the only memorable match from *Wrestlemania 13* and is undoubtedly a classic. No doubt, Hart and Michaels would have been great too but in terms of WWF's evolution at the time, the submission match was a necessary match during that time.

Hart and Austin told a magnificent story at *Wrestlemania*, and with it, both of them reversed roles that night with Austin turning face and Hart becoming the heel.

Hart and Austin would continue their rivalry for the next couple of months but despite a great story on-screen, WWF was not doing well behind-the-scenes. Ratings continued on their low-end path despite some magnificent storytelling and WWF's finances were taking a huge hit.

Despite the growing star in Austin,

McMahon couldn't yet rely on him as a big money-making draw because it was not yet proven how popular he would get, or if his popularity would fizzle out quickly. Instead, McMahon continued to rely on Michaels and Hart, especially when Michael's was cleared to wrestle again.

Hart being heel was unique because he wasn't a total heel everywhere in the world. He was mainly a heel in the states but not in the rest of the world. Because of this, McMahon devised the story to where Hart denounced America and turned pro-Canada. He would insult America in his promos and heavily promote his Canadian heritage.

In my view, as mixed opinionated as Hart is on this storyline, I loved it. I thought it was a really cool time to be a fan because it gave wrestling fans a chance to really interact with the story. Also, depending on where you were from, you either saw yourself as the heel or babyface of the story. The story lasted for about six months, but I thought it was a fun six months.

While Michaels was injured, the WWF would turn their title over to another loyal soldier, The Undertaker. Undertaker would hold the belt for five months of that year. This would lead to a brief rivalry between Hart and Undertaker, with a match scheduled at that year's *Summerslam*.

I view *Summerslam* as McMahon's test on Hart's drawing power. I think McMahon could see that the tide was changing in wrestling and fans were becoming older and weren't as interested in some of the previous draws from the company. I think *Summerslam* was a much more important event than it's remembered being, especially in Hart's case because I think the results really paved the way for what the rest of the year would be like for Hart and McMahon.

Hart had mixed opinions on the event from the start. This was arguably when Hart had the most heat with American fans and seemed to think that the storyline would continue longer into the year. However, with Michaels returning to action, the WWF decided to turn him into the heel.

The plan was set up to where Michaels would be the referee in their match and would accidentally cost The Undertaker the title. This would turn Michaels into a heel and lead into a rivalry between Undertaker and Michaels. Hart questioned this storyline because it did sort of leave him with no direction once he won the title.

The main event between Hart and Undertaker was an awesome match. Neither performer missed a beat. The ending with

Michaels went perfectly with Michaels hitting Undertaker with a chair and Hart getting the win.

After this, it was becoming clear, even as a fan watching, that something strange was going on with Hart's character and something was up backstage. The WWF seemed perfectly content for the next few months centering its attention on Undertaker and Michaels but kind of left Hart on the back-burner with a lackluster feud with the Patriot that went on for only a couple months. It was obvious that WWF was just using Hart as a carrier of the championship until he dropped it to Michaels.

On the backstage end of it, things were self-destructing in the WWF. Ratings were not improving and WWF was reportedly in "financial peril". This culminated in a meeting between Hart and McMahon where it was laid out that McMahon could no longer afford Hart's twenty-year contract and requested him to seek his old offer from WCW.

McMahon has gone on record in stating that he told Hart that he would live up to the contract if Hart stayed but also laid out his creative plans for the next year for WWF, which did not include Hart. Hart ultimately elected to bow out of their deal and seek his offer from WCW.

All discussions with Eric Bischoff and

Hart began in September. Bischoff, by that time, was in more need of Hart than he was a year earlier. Bischoff had been given orders to start plans for a new show on TBS for WCW called *Thunder*. Due to the lack of talent to support the new show, he would need another big name to help promote the show and saw Hart as the big name he needed.

It was because of this that Hart was able to secure his deal very easily. On the other hand, he was also hoping that the deal would fall through. He had no intentions of leaving the company, even with the lackluster creative plans for him. He did not see himself leaving the WWF. Much to his surprise, the deal was finalized in only a few weeks.

On-screen, Hart and Michaels had entered into a rivalry with each other that was set to culminate at *Survivor Serious* in Montreal, Canada. The storyline was initially set up to be Hart's last match with the WWF, even though it had not yet been made public that he was leaving.

It was written that Hart would drop the belt to Michaels at *Survivor Series* because it was reported that Hart's contract would be expired by the end of that night. There have been some conflicting stories that his contract didn't end until the following month, but the latter has never been proven in writing.

Hart refused to lose to Michaels at *Survivor Series*, which caused quite an uproar. Hart was actually within his legal right to refuse this because he had complete creative control in his last month with the company. McMahon however, continued to push Hart to drop the belt at *Survivor Series* due to his fear of Hart showing up with the belt on WCW *Nitro*.

Both Hart and Bischoff have gone on record that there was no way that the belt would be brought on television due to the legality of it. WWF and WCW were in the midst of a court case, which stemmed back to Bischoff having Madusa drop the WWF's Women's Championship in the trash on *Nitro*. WCW was on the losing end of that case and Bischoff didn't want to worsen the matter.

Besides, Bischoff was also fully aware that he no longer had to go that far with his tactics. WCW was well ahead in the ratings by that point and had no need for dirty tactics.

McMahon was not convinced, and continued to pressure Hart and pressured him all the way up until *Survivor Series*.

Hart has been criticized by many within the industry because of his unwillingness to lose the title in Canada. Legends like Ted Debiase and Ric Flair feel that it was poor sportsmanship on his part for not wanting to drop the title before his departure. I'll buy into Debiase's argument, but Flair should be the last person accusing anybody of anything.

I think a lot of it had to do with Hart's pride for the most part. Hart was a very prideful man and was viewed as a hero in Canada. Hart also stated around this time that he would have rather come out of the wrestling business as a success rather than a tragedy, which is very much what many wrestlers end up being.

I think Hart viewed losing in Montreal in his final match to a man that he viewed as disrespectful to the wrestling industry as the ultimate slap in the face. In many ways I see where Hart is coming from, and seeing how loved he was as a wrestling traditionalist and how his career had evolved, it was understandable to see his point-of-view.

While McMahon and Hart argued about the ending, McMahon was discussing the ending with others around him when Hart was not around. The night before *Survivor Series* there was a meeting between McMahon, Gerald Brisco, Shawn Michaels, and Triple H. The meeting took place in McMahon's hotel room.

McMahon explained the situation of Hart not wanting to lose at *Survivor Series* and wanted to know how to get out of this situation. According to Michaels, he really had no firm answers and McMahon basically beat around the bush. He stated that it was Triple H who chimed in with, "Fuck him, if he won't do business, you do business for him."

With that said, the plans were laid out for the *screwjob*. Hart and Michaels had already laid out the basics for the match earlier that day. At some point within the match, Hart gave Michaels permission to put Hart's classic finisher, *The Sharpshooter*, on Hart himself. McMahon decided to use this moment as the moment to screw Hart. Referee Earl Hebner would get up after being knocked down from a collision with Hart and Michaels and would immediately call for the bell, although Hart had not submitted.

These were the plans laid out and according to both Michaels and Triple H, they were specifically told to deny any knowledge of the events and leave McMahon to take all of the blame, so they didn't damage their careers.

Hart reportedly became very suspicious of McMahon's actions when the *Survivor Series* kicked off the next night because McMahon would not be doing commentary that night, which was very unusual back then. McMahon and Hart met earlier that night to discuss the plans for the match.

McMahon, within the course of the meeting, proceeded to acknowledge his respect and thankfulness for Hart and all that he had done with the company and also acknowledging Hart's plans for the match. Hart requested the match to end by disqualification and he would forfeit the title the very next night live on *Raw*. McMahon verbally agreed to the terms that Hart had laid out, leaving Hart to believe that the match would be a disqualification ending.

While Hart was convinced, his family and friends were not. His brother, Owen, and fellow wrestler, Vader, both warned him to be aware of any sort of screwjob McMahon may be planning. They warned him not to stay down too long and avoid fast counts by the referee.

Hart was mainly convinced due to referee Earl Hebner. Hebner and Hart were well-known friends and Hebner had given his word that he wouldn't allow anything to happen. In Hebner's defense, he wasn't aware of the events until just before the match started, and it was either do it or possibly lose his job, so he wasn't in a great position.

When the match took place, it was rather odd to watch on television. As a fan, you could sense that something was going on. There was so much security around the ring and

McMahon was actually at ringside in a suit, which was the first time he had ever been out there in that attire and not behind the announce table.

Hart also visibly broke character a few times during the match, showing his suspicion of McMahon and also showing some disdain to some of the audience. While Hart was greeted overwhelmingly well by the Canadian crowd, word of his departure leaked to some of the general public and that small group of fans voiced their disappointment to Bret, which he became noticeably disturbed by.

It came off close to reality television for a few moments throughout it. You could just feel that something big was brewing but didn't know what it was until it happened. When the screwjob finally did happen, it was so quick that you have to really pay attention in order to take it in because the event went off the air only twenty seconds after it happened.

The crowd on hand was very aware of the events that transpired and proceeded to chant "bullshit" and some even threw trash in the ring. The last twenty seconds of the event were memorable mainly because it just managed to catch Hart spitting in McMahon's face.

After the event went off the air, Hart proceeded to break equipment and vent all of his frustrations in front of the sold out crowd. When he was finally able to go backstage, everyone that was back there just stood in shock over what had happened.

Reportedly, The Undertaker went to McMahon's office and banged on the locked door and told McMahon to apologize to Hart. By the time McMahon got to the locker room, Hart had already confronted Michaels, who stated that he had no idea what had happened and had no prior knowledge. Hart could only take this at face value because he didn't know whether it was true or not.

When McMahon got to the locker room, he tried to explain his actions and why he did what he did. He invited Hart to vent his frustrations on him, which led to Hart punching McMahon in the face. Before things could escalate any further, Hart ordered McMahon to leave, which he obliged.

Hart's wife at the time, Julie, confronted Triple H while Hart, Michaels, and McMahon were in the locker room. Triple H, like Michaels, denied all knowledge.

Years after the incident, many insiders and fans have looked back on the screwjob (now dubbed *The Montreal Screwjob*) and have begun discussing it and questioning its legitimacy.

From my standpoint, I think the actions

that the WWF took on Hart at the *Survivor Series* were very real. However, I'm very inclined to disbelieve McMahon's end of the story and the WWF's supposed financial state.

I think McMahon was looking for any excuse to get out of his deal with Hart. McMahon knew that he had nothing to offer Hart, and knew that the WWF could no longer rely on him as a top talent, especially when looking at the direction that he wanted to take the company.

McMahon was already in negotiations with the New York Stock Exchange on taking the WWF public. Taking the company public meant that he would have to cut short every long-term deal he had under the company's payroll, and his longest term was Hart and their one and a half million dollars a year deal for twenty years.

I don't think it was as much the WWF being in financial peril, as it was McMahon wanting to cut Hart from his roster, leaving one and a half million he could save per year to give to the talent that he would need over the next couple of years.

WWF being private at the time makes it very tough to determine their actual financial state because they were not required to release any transactions to the public. In fact, up until that point, only two transactions were ever made public, their signing of Brian Pillman in 1996 and Bret Hart's twenty-year deal.

This made WWF's claim of financial difficulties very questionable. It's especially become questionable over time when you look back at the big picture on the WWF product back in 1997.

While the ratings in the states were low, the WWF were drawing big in the house show market because they were the only ones doing house shows because WCW refused to do so at the time. The attendance for their live and taped shows was up from 1996, and they were able to boost their production budget for *Raw* in order to revamp the show and make it more competitive with WCW's product.

The biggest advantage in WWF's corner when compared to WCW was their global presence. One thing that WCW never had that WWF firmly grasped onto was their global market. WWF had a huge global following, to the point where their numbers more than quadrupled WCW's numbers.

When you look at the WWF's production from that standpoint, it's very hard to believe that they were in any financial danger. True, they might not have had the budget of WCW, but I think they were much more well off than they were letting on.

It also doesn't defend their claim anymore when you consider that only two months later, they entered a multi-million dollar deal with Mike Tyson, but we'll get to that later.

One quote that will always stick with me from McMahon was the quote he made on Hart's documentary, *Wrestling with Shadows*. McMahon says in the documentary, "I think I was sorry that I signed a deal. Bret had leveraged himself against Turner's operation and bid himself up so much that everyone around me was saying 'No, you can't let Bret go.' I listened to them, I think I'm sorry that I did."

A lot of people confuse that last line where McMahon says "I think I'm sorry that I did", and think that he's apologizing for letting Hart go. He's actually apologizing for listening to the people that told him to keep Hart. So, I think there was a deep regret on McMahon's part of keeping Hart from the beginning when he returned after *Wrestlemania XII*.

I think McMahon was blinded by the fact that so many of his talent were choosing to leave for WCW, that he bid so much into keeping Hart on his roster and bid way more than he wanted to in the end. I think McMahon saw that he overpaid for a wrestler that he didn't need. So overall, I'm a firm believer that he lied to Hart to get him to leave.

WCW was at a high in the creative department and it was showing in their ratings. WCW was winning by a landslide in all of 1997. They had a major heel faction in the NWO and their rivalry between Hulk Hogan and Sting was turning out to be one of the greatest rivalries in wrestling history.

There is nothing negative you can say about Eric Bischoff during this time. He mapped out this rivalry perfectly and what made it so perfect was the fact that it would take a year and a half for Hogan and Sting to even have a match. It was the perfect, slow-moving process that we do not see anymore because everything is just quick and to the point now.

This was one of those rivalries where chemistry was everything. Hogan, up to that point, I think had a lot of trouble finding chemistry with a lot of the veteran WCW players, which is what I think hindered a lot of his early years with the company, from a long-term storyline perspective. With Sting, he found an instant bond.

Sting was one of those performers who could work with anyone, whether they were young or old. Sting was a lot like Bret Hart in many ways. He was someone who could bring the best out of even the most limited wrestler, even a wrestler as limited as Hogan.

Hogan and Sting's rivalry relied a lot on theatrics, especially with Sting's character. He would look down from the rafters and would be repelled down to attack various members of the NWO, including Hogan.

Sting's character was the greatest contrast to the NWO. This was a character and man who bled WCW. He was someone who had been with the company through its highs and lows. Now he was an almost vigilante-like character out to destroy the enemies of WCW, the NWO.

The story, while being fiction, felt very personal and that's what made it intriguing. You felt that there was something to gain and something to lose for both characters, which you rarely feel from pro wrestling. Again, all of these feelings were because of this masterful storytelling process that Bischoff and his creative team had written up and it was coming off perfectly on-screen.

The storyline had generated so much interest from the fans that it didn't matter what the WWF did at that time, most fans just wanted to see how the Hogan and Sting rivalry was going to end.

WCW seemed to have the perfect

opportunity to eclipse the WWF with their annual event, *Starrcade* in 1997. This would be the match that all fans were waiting for. Hogan and Sting would finally face-off and WCW marketed the hell out of it.

From the start of the rivalry, the ending seemed to be set in stone. It would be this long back and forth rivalry, with Sting coming out on top cleanly in the end.

There was just one problem with this ending and it was the fact that it involved Hogan. Hogan doesn't like anyone coming out on top cleanly over him. This was another one of those occasions where Hogan's creative control played a huge role.

The ending to the match all seemed to be set to take place as planned from the beginning until that very night at *Starrcade*. According to Hogan, he was not impressed with Sting and felt that he wasn't committed to the storyline. This all came about on how Sting looked apparently.

Sting was rarely seen, beyond his appearances on *Nitro*, by anybody. The man behind the character, Steve Borden, was going through a lot of personal issues by 1997. He was admittedly going through a lot of alcohol and substance abuse. At one point, there was even admittance to adultery on Borden's part during this time.

Borden was trying everything to cure himself during this time, as well as being on television every week for the storyline.

Borden had not wrestled in the ring for the entire time this rivalry was underway, so he was not really needed beyond the capacity that WCW was using him at with his character Sting. He would just show up, do his character and leave.

So apparently, when he arrived at the MCI Center that night, Hogan was not impressed with his appearance. According to Bischoff, he looked out of shape, not tanned, and didn't appear committed.

Hogan would walk over to Bischoff, and in only so many words, would say to Bischoff that he wasn't buying into Sting's character as the top guy. Because Hogan had such massive stroke creatively, Bischoff had to scramble to change everything to Hogan's liking.

Starrcade took place on December 28, 1997, only a month and a half after WWF's *Survivor Series*, where Bret Hart was legitimately screwed out of his title and the WWF. Hart had just started appearing on WCW's broadcast only two weeks before *Starrcade*. Hart was not cleared to wrestle due to a sixty day no compete clause from his WWF contract. So, Hart was written to be the referee for a few matches.

Hart served as the referee for a match between Eric Bischoff and Larry Zbysko. This was written to be Hart's only appearance at *Starrcade* at first. However, with Bischoff needing to come up with an ending for the match with Hogan and Sting, he decided to include Hart in the main event.

Sting would still be set to win the title but not in the clean manner initially discussed. The story was written to where Hogan would pin Sting and referee Nick Patrick would fast count Sting, screwing Sting in the match. Bischoff meant for this to cash in on the *Montreal Screwjob*, which seemed fitting since Hart was now in WCW.

After this, Hart would stop the timekeeper from ringing the bell and would restart the match, allowing Sting to make a comeback and win the title.

With all things considered and knowing that this was a last minute decision, this wasn't a bad idea by Bischoff and seemed as though it could pay off.

Unfortunately, things didn't go as planned as Nick Patrick did not fast count like he was supposed to. Instead, he made a regular count. Hart still went according to plan and restarted the match. While everything else did go as planned and Sting won the match, that one botch by Patrick ruined the entire thing.

WCW tried to save the angle as best they could, but they couldn't hide the fact that they screwed up royally on live television. To make matters worse, Sting didn't even attempt to kick out of Hogan's pin, which definitely would have saved everything if Sting kicked out at two and Patrick still counted to three.

The main event was just bizarre overall. You got a sense of legit hatred between Hogan and Sting, which was probably literally there. There have been so many rumors on this and I think some hold truth to what happened that night and others don't.

Most of the outcome purely lies on Hogan's shoulders. Hogan's excuse for not wanting to lose to Sting cleanly was the most ludicrous thing I have ever heard. I think Hogan legitimately felt threatened by Sting and didn't want Sting to be bigger than him.

The whole story of Sting looking out of shape was clearly a lie on both Hogan and Bischoff's part. Sting, in my opinion, looked awesome that night and wrestled perfectly, especially considering he had taken off from in-ring action for a quite a while since the storyline began.

I'm most likely very wrong on this but I always viewed Sting not kicking out during the three count as intentional by Sting himself. I felt that moment was the moment where it looked like Sting just wanted to bury the angle.

If that were the case, it would be understandable. Sting had been informed almost from the start that he would be the clear winner in the entire rivalry, and to be told only hours before the match took place that plans had changed couldn't have been a great thing to hear.

Sting has gone on record that he didn't care about the outcome in general because he was just there to have a good match. I'm very inclined not to believe him on that, but unless he says different, we'll never really know. Only he can be the one to clear up what really happened that night. We've already gotten one side of the story, we just need the other.

Chapter XV
Thunder and an Overstretched Production

In late 1997, Eric Bischoff was pulled into a meeting with Ted Turner. Turner announced that he wanted to kick off another WCW show on TBS titled *Thunder*. It would air every week on Thursday nights.

I think Turner's decision for *Thunder* was driven by the fact that wrestling was initially housed by TBS and was one of his first big money-making productions on his network when it started. I think Turner always saw a home for wrestling on TBS and while he knew he couldn't move *Nitro* from TNT due to its success, he felt that he could create a new product for TBS and bring close to, if not the same success.

Bischoff was very reluctant to comply, marking the first time that he had ever questioned any of Turner's decisions. But it was him versus his billionaire boss, so there was no discussing it with Turner. He was given his orders and that was it.

I think a lot of insiders overlooked the reason on why Bischoff was so hesitant. People have to remember that WCW was not run like the WWF at the time. They didn't have house shows and only had a secondary taped show in their Saturday broadcast. They didn't have nearly as big of a crew as the WWF, especially when it came to running multiple shows.

Bischoff had to stretch beyond his means to get the production setup for *Thunder*, including pulling new production crew members from Turner Broadcasting to fill the crew he needed.

Another issue was the talent. Bischoff's fear was that having two shows would water down the talent's on-screen presence and any storylines that they were in. So, he felt he needed to run *Thunder* as an almost separate entity from *Nitro*. While the bigger storylines would be run through both shows, for the most part, some of the smaller ones would be on one or the other. As stated before, this was one of the biggest reasons why WCW needed Bret Hart at the time.

The biggest obstacle for Bischoff was TBS itself. Producers with TBS refused to fund *Thunder*. There have been many theories on this, but I think the most accurate was the bitterness that the rest of Turner Broadcasting had for WCW.

WCW was once viewed as the redheaded stepchild of the entire company. Many within Turner flat out rejected it and to see WCW end up being the top broadcast in the company created a lot of jealousy and I think there was jealousy when it was announced that WCW was moving back to TBS because it instantly toppled over every other show in terms of value.

So I think in an aggressive nature, TBS let WCW produce their own show as if to say "We don't care that you're here." TBS's lack of funding left WCW with a ten to fifteen million dollar per year production cost for *Thunder*.

In order to compensate that, Bischoff decided to rev up the house shows for WCW again. This did not go well with the big names in WCW. Many of the bigger names in WCW including Hogan, Nash, Hall, Sting, Goldberg, and more felt that they were already doing Bischoff a favor by appearing on the new show.

Also, for guys like Hogan, their contracts stated that they were only to be on WCW programming for a limited time per year, so none of their contracts included house shows and they weren't obligated to any changes that may be made for everyone else.

I can honestly say that WCW's house shows were probably the most uneventful shows on the face of the planet. I went to see one of their house shows in early 1999 in Utica, New York. With no big names in the show, a lot of the show was filled with contracted WCW wrestlers that weren't big enough to appear on either *Nitro* or *Thunder*. Granted there were some big names like Bam Bam Bigelow and even Booker T took part of a few of them but they weren't as spectacular or well-received as the WWF's house shows.

It was very clear that WCW was not trying to do anything extravagant with their house shows or do anything that would compete with WWF like *Nitro* or *Thunder*. The house shows were just meant for revenues, particularly for WCW *Thunder*.

When *Thunder* went on the air on January 8, 1998, it was a great show by itself and I say it very specifically that way because that's pretty much what it was. While *Thunder* was a good show, it was always stuck in the shadow of *Nitro* and never really seemed to be taken as seriously as *Nitro*. It just couldn't get out of that b-show stigma.

Chapter XVI
Stone Cold, Mike Tyson, Undertaker, and Wrestlemania XIV

WCW's stress over budget and failure with *Starrcade* could not have come at a worse time as WWF began to close the gap and was playing a more aggressive game.

WWF's slow transition began to really take shape in late 1997, with McMahon finally ready to place Steve Austin in a more prominent role on the program. Austin was proving to be a massive draw for the company with his merchandise sales beginning to eclipse everyone in the industry. The ironic part was that it was all over the simplest t-shirt ever and that being the original Austin 3:16 shirt.

Austin's on-screen presence was nearly doubled by the end of 1997 versus his on-screen time just earlier in the year. Austin's brash attitude, foul-mouth, finger gesturing, and beer drinking persona was becoming the new hero to wrestling fans.

Despite what people might think, Austin's face turn was not totally complete after *Wrestlemania 13*. It was still a slow build-up throughout the rest of the year because fans were still warming up to him being in the babyface role.

I think one the reasons why it was such a slow build for Austin was because he wasn't the typical babyface. He was really the first of his kind because he was a babyface that would do heel tactics. He was a guy that not only attacked the heels but would attack the other babyfaces if he wanted to, but that's what slowly made him cool to watch.

Another reason for Austin's slow rise, in my opinion, was because of McMahon. I think there was hesitation on McMahon's and the rest of the creative team's part. There seemed to be a level of uneasiness on whether or not placing him in the babyface role was a good idea.

In fact, according to Austin, the creative team did try to step in on a lot of his on-screen actions. They tried to get him to tone down his language and to get him to not use the middle finger. Austin countered by saying "I'm not for everybody", and I think that spoke volumes on how he wanted to roll with the character. It was a babyface character that was still a heel by his personality traits but steadily became cool.

I think if Austin had given in to the demands of the creative team, the character would have fallen flat.

Unfortunately, the rise of his character almost came to a crashing end in the summer

WWF was approaching its annual event, *Summerslam,* and Austin was in a heated rivalry with Owen Hart. Hart and Austin's rivalry kicked off almost immediately after his feud with Owen's brother Bret.

The feud was originally slated to be a shorter rivalry with *Summerslam* being one of two matches they would have. The stipulation of the match was that if Austin won, he won the Intercontinental title, but if he lost, he would have to kiss Hart's ass.

Austin was scheduled to win the match. During their discussions for the match, they decided that Hart would go for a Tombstone Piledriver. The Tombstone was actually the finishing move of The Undertaker's but Hart would execute it differently to make it appear like a different maneuver.

The Tombstone is generally a move executed by bigger wrestlers like Undertaker. The reason for this is because it requires a lot of strength and balance to pull off.

The match between Hart and Austin went smoothly. There wasn't quite the chemistry between Austin and Owen as there was with Austin and Bret but it was still a well-executed match. The spot came for the Tombstone and as soon as Hart picked up Austin, everyone who saw Austin's head placement knew that it was marked for disaster.

Hart dropped straight into a sitting position, driving Austin head first into the mat. Everyone in the arena and watching on television knew that something went wrong because Austin went still and Hart stalled for several minutes.

Austin lost feeling in all of his body for a bit but managed to regain feeling and pin Hart for the win.

Austin was out of action for two months, which was a nightmare for WWF, because just as they were catching ground, their rising star was injured.

Austin did some segments while out of the ring recovering and seeing doctors to keep him present on-screen. When he was good to travel again, he began appearing in the arena's live on *Raw* but still not wrestling any matches. He finally returned at *Survivor Series* in a short rematch with Hart, winning the Intercontinental title again.

Despite the injury and Austin's limited wrestling style due to it, he continued to grow in popularity. It was getting to the point where the crowds were deafening when he entered the arena. As 1998 approached, with WWF's ratings beginning to rise, McMahon knew that Austin was next in line to lead his company.

Several major storylines were kick-started

in late 1997 that would transition into 1998. They had The Undertaker and Kane, Undertaker and Shawn Michaels, and Stone Cold and Vince McMahon. The latter wouldn't really pick-up speed until after *Wrestlemania XIV* but was generally hinted at in the latter part of 1997.

Austin was set to win the *Royal Rumble* and Michaels was set to win the WWF title, leading to their match at *Wrestlemania*. Rumors have swerved, after the fact that Michaels and Austin were to go longer into the year with a possible rematch or two. However, before things could pan out, Michaels would be injured at the *Royal Rumble*, which would leave him out of action until his match with Austin at *Wrestlemania*, which would end up being his last match for over four years.

To Michael's credit, he remained on television for the entire storyline, which wound up being a great one. To add to the storyline and the WWF's slowly changing attitude, the WWF signed Mike Tyson to be part of the story as well.

Tyson was a hot commodity at the time; he was recently suspended from Boxing due to his match with Evander Holyfield, which resulted in Tyson biting off part of Holyfield's ear. Tyson had so much heat because of his suspension and was such an outspoken person, that he seemed perfect with the WWF from a publicity standpoint.

He came onto the show on January 19, 1998, to a sea of boos. What seemed to be a basic interview wound up being interrupted by Austin. He and Tyson then got into what is the best publicity stunt I've ever seen from the WWF and current WWE. Austin gave Tyson the finger and Tyson shoved Austin, which led to sheer pandemonium in the ring.

The stunt was so big, that every newspaper, sports broadcaster, journalist, and news show mentioned it the very next day. The execution by the WWF was perfect and couldn't have gone anymore in their favor.

Tyson was a great asset to McMahon and the WWF. He was the right person, at the right place, at the right time. The WWF needed someone to get them back into the thick of things, and he was the one to do it.

Another storyline that was running at the time, which I actually think was just as good, if not better than Austin and Michael's was The Undertaker and Kane.

The storyline had actually kicked off shortly after Undertaker won the title at *Wrestlemania 13*. The story started with Paul Bearer, Undertaker's former manager, claiming that Undertaker's brother Kane, who was believed to be dead, was alive and wanting revenge.

This storyline built for several months, with Kane (being played by Glenn Jacobs) making his debut at *Badd Blood* during the first ever Hell in the Cell match, and costing Undertaker the match.

The Undertaker stood his ground on not wanting to fight his brother, until being pushed over the edge at the *Royal Rumble* and finally accepting his brother's challenge.

This story was just so well written and there weren't two better big men to take the story on than Undertaker and Kane, and Kane being the silent enemy with Bearer as his mouthpiece was genius.

I think what made this storyline so unique was the length of time it took to finally result in a match. Much like Hogan and Sting at WCW, the WWF prolonged the match between the two. However, the big difference here was that Kane didn't make his debut until almost five months after the story began.

Undertaker was probably McMahon's most loyal soldier at the time in terms of storyline involvement because he was a part of other storylines while the one with Kane was still being built as well, including with wrestlers like Farooq, Steve Austin, Bret Hart, and Shawn Michaels. He was pulling a lot of double-duty without a single complaint.

All-in-all, the WWF had two very powerful storylines leading them to *Wrestlemania XIV*. There was so much press coverage with Tyson, and a lot of fan interest building with Austin, Michaels, Taker, and Kane. Not only that but the smaller storylines were also brewing with Mick Foley and Terry Funk facing off with the New Age Outlaws (Jesse James and Billy Gunn) and there was also a great mid-card rivalry between Triple H and Owen Hart.

As *Wrestlemania* loomed closer, it was clear that something big was brewing, and I think it really sunk in for me that *Wrestlemania* was going to be big when McMahon actually cleared a timeslot on NBC for a *Wrestlemania* press conference.

It was rare that wrestling ever did press conferences, and to see one by the WWF, on NBC no less, was amazing.

While things were looking up for *Wrestlemania*, things weren't looking up for their main event match. As I stated earlier, Michael's was injured, which resulted in a major rewriting of the story. However, Michael's back injury was causing him severe aggravation, and was also causing him to become very frustrated with certain small things. For instance, during an event titled the *DX Public Workout,* Michaels, Triple H, Chyna, and Mike Tyson stood in front of a large crowd of thirteen thousand people and were ready to promote the event when someone hit Michaels with a battery. Because of this, Michaels just plain walked out.

With Michaels temperament and *Wrestlemania* looming very close, it was unclear if Michaels would do the honors for Austin and actually let him win. There have been rumors that Michaels was threatened by The Undertaker to do everything as planned, but there hasn't been any true confirmation of the incident beyond rumors.

Wrestlemania XIV could not have gone any better for the company. Because of all the media attention from Tyson, the well-built storylines for most of its mid-card and all of its main event matches, it turned out to be WWF's most watched event in several years and generated a bunch of money for the company.

As a fan watching it on television, you could tell that it was going to be a game changer for the company, even with Michaels leaving after it was over. Things were changing and it was all for the better.

Chapter XVII
Raw Begins to Make Strides, WCW Bring in Goldberg, but Faces Standards and Practices

McMahon was smart enough to see that things were looking up and wanted to keep the momentum going for the WWF. He cut a promo with Austin the next night, which in my view kicked off the Austin/McMahon rivalry officially. A lot of people believed that it kicked off in October of 1997 but I don't think it really did. There were small spots during that time but I think this was the one that let everyone know that it was on at that point.

The Austin/McMahon rivalry has been highlighted as the rivalry that saved the WWF, but I think it was more than that. Austin and McMahon did more of a promo rivalry than a match one. There weren't many five-star matches at the time with Austin and whomever he faced during that time. They were good matches but Austin's popularity and his chemistry with McMahon during promos was what really drove the WWF forward.

On April 13, the WWF decided to headline *Raw* with a match between Austin and McMahon. I remember watching this *Raw* live when it happened and it's often been sighted as a pivotal moment in the rivalry between WWF and WCW. I know it was the night that *Raw* beat *Nitro* for the first time in eighty-four weeks, but in all honesty, it wasn't that great of a main event match and I believe it wasn't as great as so many remember it being.

I think the fact that it was the first *Raw* episode to beat *Nitro* in nearly two years overshadowed the fact that it was a subpar main event at best. Essentially, WWF pulled the same bait and switch concept that would get WCW in trouble later on. They promoted a main event that was to have Austin and McMahon wrestle for the first time.

They spent the entire two-hour show promoting this match, only to have it interrupted by Dude Love (Mick Foley), which resulted in one of the most cluttered conclusions to *Raw* that I can remember. To the WWF's credit, it did lead to a very good storyline between Austin and Foley, which was short but sweet, but the overall *Raw* episode that beat *Nitro* was overblown after it aired and didn't deserve to be.

Raw would continue to get bolder as time went on. Stone Cold's character was also becoming bolder with him drinking beer on an almost weekly basis, and with his language getting more colorful over time. However, the big shift was with WWF's sexual content.

The USA Network had tried to keep the WWF at bay when things were starting to get a little more extreme but were beginning to see the shift in the ratings and decided to give the WWF almost complete full reign in what they could do. Obviously, the WWF still had a line that they couldn't cross but it was much farther away than it had been a year before.

The WWF's sexual content had started a year and a half prior with the character of Sunny being introduced. They dressed her up sexy for the cameras and made her appeal to the older male demographic. Things would be taken further with Sable. Sable was first introduced in 1996. She was already known to be a very beautiful woman but the WWF wanted to push it to the unknown limits at the time.

They had her dressing as revealing as possible and having her do grinds and other sexual gestures in the ring.

Another thing that was going on as well was D-Generation X. The group had initially started with just Shawn Michaels, Triple H, and Chyna, but after Michael's left due to injury, the group expanded with Triple H, Chyna, X-Pac, Road Dogg, and Billy Gunn. DX was known for their comedy, which was very much a cross between college humor and just plain toilet humor.

Not only was the content of the show changing but the wrestling was too. The days of long and grueling matches seemed to be in the past (except for main event pay-per-view matches) and were made shorter and to the point.

This had a lot to do with WWF's Head Writer during that time, Vince Russo. Russo believed in a concept that has become known as *Crash TV*. This is where the show becomes far faster paced, and rivalries are kept short and sweet, and promos and segments become more controversial. Russo loved this style of storytelling and it was the type of storytelling that WWF needed.

WCW needed a retaliation to the WWF's changing attitude and they seemed to find it in former football player Bill Goldberg. Goldberg had played for a few years with the NFL, his highest profile stint being with the Atlanta Falcons until injuries took him out of the sport.

Goldberg was invited to WCW's training camp (known as the Power Plant) and was easily impressive due to his size and strength. Bischoff was so impressed with him that he was brought on television for his first match on September 22, 1997, and would begin his famous undefeated streak.

Goldberg's undefeated streak was the

thing that brought him to the dance and really made him stand out amongst fans. He was written to be this unstoppable force that would come out, beat his opponent within a matter of minutes and would be done for the night. In fact, Goldberg's elaborate entrance was longer than most of his matches. He felt very much like The Ultimate Warrior in terms of setup.

Goldberg's timing could not have been better for WCW because they were in need of a new star and not just established stars. The only issue with Goldberg was his experience. He had the size, strength, and agility, but lacked the in-ring knowledge to put on a technical match.

There were brief matches where Bischoff wanted to test Goldberg, for instance, his match with William Regal in February of 1998, which has become infamous for showing Goldberg's lack of wrestling ability, so it became pretty clear that they couldn't do that with Goldberg and had to keep things simple.

I think WCW, especially Bischoff, were very aware that they had to push Goldberg quickly because there wasn't really enough character or depth within Goldberg's arsenal to drag the character out. The character didn't quite have the longevity of guys like Bret Hart, Austin, Hogan, etc...

It was in this case that it was decided that Goldberg would win the World Title. According to Bischoff, the idea of Goldberg winning the title was all Hogan's, which can go either way of being true or not, but it was decided that Goldberg would win the title on July 6, 1998, live on *Nitro*.

The match would take place in Goldberg's hometown of Atlanta, Georgia in the Georgia Dome, in front of over forty-thousand people. By July of that year, WWF and WCW were usually going back and forth in the ratings, but things were starting to lean in the WWF's favor with the Austin/McMahon rivalry and edgier storylines.

Bischoff decided to use every bit of promotional power that WCW had to promote the championship match between Goldberg and Hogan, trying to get as much viewership as they could muster for the show, and it was needed for WCW. The really interesting part about it was that it was actually a match that wasn't guaranteed to happen storyline-wise because Goldberg had to beat Scott Hall in a match that very same night of the championship match in order to actually have the match. Fans weren't fooled; they knew it was going to happen regardless because of Goldberg's undefeated streak.

One of the common criticism's that has

been thrown Bischoff's way for this show was placing a pay-per-view quality match on free television, but I think it was probably the smartest thing they could have done at the time.

As great as pay-per-view buyrates were to wrestling during that time, there was never a chance to get a match in front of as many eyes as possible other than *Nitro* or *Raw*. Pay-per-views for wrestling in the 90s' and even most of the 2000s' hovered from anywhere between one hundred thousand to four hundred thousand buys, which usually meant it was seen by, at most, one million people, maybe a little over.

When hosting a match on *Nitro* or *Raw*, especially in 1998 or 1999, the match could be viewed by anywhere from four million to seven million people, so it was a big difference. What also made Bischoff's decision more understandable was the fact that WCW's buyrates, despite their television ratings, were never really great. They did have a couple great buyrate numbers in 1997 and 1998, but their pay-per-view buyrates never tended to match the WWF's as far as consistency.

It was actually a really good *Nitro* that WCW put on that night and the crowd was red hot for Goldberg. Just the intensity and atmosphere of the event made a great *Nitro* to watch. While Goldberg's matches with both Hall and Hogan weren't great, it was easily made up for by the crowd.

It was also very cool to see a title change of that magnitude happen on regular television, which made it all the more important. WCW definitely did themselves a favor with this show because it did stop WWF's momentum temporarily, which is what they were looking for.

It was at this point that I felt that WCW should have capitalized a whole lot better than they did. They had a hot superstar in Goldberg, who was now champion, so the show should have been revolved around him and his championship reign. This didn't happen as WCW still felt it best to focus primarily on Hogan.

Shortly after losing the title, Hogan and Bischoff decided to go for a more mainstream storyline to help grow their audience even further. Since WCW was owned by Turner Broadcasting, they had a lot of political power when it came to celebrity appearances. They had used this power to get celebrities into matches in the past, my favorite being Dennis Rodman and Karl Malone. I never imagined that those two would be good wrestlers but they did really well.

Because it had proven to be so successful

in the past, WCW decided to do it again, this time with...Jay Leno. No, that's not a typo, WCW made a deal with Jay Leno and to have him in a match. It would be Diamond Dallas Page and Jay Leno facing Hulk Hogan and Eric Bischoff.

This whole storyline started with Jay Leno poking fun of wrestling on his show, Hogan and Bischoff then appear and continue to argue with Leno over it. At one point, Bischoff and Hogan took over Leno's show and it actually was rather hilarious. Overall, it was just a meaningless storyline and a lame publicity stunt by Bischoff.

It was a storyline that I think just hurt Goldberg's reign as champion. He should have been their focus, and yet at their next pay-per-view, *Road Wild*, they had Goldberg in a semi-main event battle royal, with his title not even on the line. He was the semi-main to the main event, which was the tag match with Jay Leno.

Something was wrong with Goldberg's first reign and it reeked of Hogan's creative control, but I could be wrong and it might have just been a poor call by Bischoff. Either way, it was a terrible way to go for a rising star like Goldberg.

To make matters worse, directly after *Road Wild*, Bischoff was called into a meeting at Turner Broadcasting. This meeting would be with the newly formed Standards and Practices department at Turner. This department had stemmed from Turner's merger with Time Warner.

I'll touch on the merger briefly. In 1996, Turner was looking to grow his business. He saw a great opportunity with Time Warner. Time Warner had shown their interest in acquiring Turner Broadcasting and *merging* with Turner. I put merging in italic because that's the impression that Turner had at the time of the deal.

Turner had his agenda when he merged with Time Warner and it was to keep doing what he was doing. However, Time Warner had their agenda as well and it did not involve Turner. Time Warner's intention was to slowly but surely push Turner out of office. However, because of Turner's power in the entertainment world, and being the lead stockholder, they could not do this easily. So they slowly forced their hand into each section of the company, trying to undermine Turner. One of their first stops was WCW.

Time Warner had their own vision of TBS and TNT and it didn't involve WCW, so they were trying to find ways to phase the company out. Their first step was Standards and Practices, which was a department that no one at Turner Broadcasting prior to the merger, had ever heard of, including Bischoff.

Bischoff sat in a room with a bunch of people that he didn't know and the first thing that they said to him was that his show had to be for *families.*

While most shows might not have thought much of this demand, it was the last thing that Bischoff wanted to hear period. WCW had always been for an older demographic and that was the audience it had been catering to since Bischoff joined the company and was successful at doing so.

They stated that he would need to turn in all scripts for his shows and that they would need to be reviewed before any of their shows went into production.

All of these requests were out of line for a wrestling show. While many storylines were planned out in advance, a lot of the promos and matches were not really planned until the day of or night before. Even if they were planned in advanced, they weren't scripted. Wrestling shows at the time were more like bullet points. They were planned and usually written down to only give short examples of what they wanted, but it was the wrestler that brought it to life and not the words written on paper.

All of these provisions were made to WCW

and Bischoff has stated that it didn't sound like they even knew what the show was about, and couldn't even tell him what night of the week they aired. So something strange was going on and it was clear that Time Warner was behind it all.

Chapter XVIII
Warrior and Halloween Havoc

Almost directly after the meeting with Standards and Practices, WCW would work out a deal with wrestling legend, The Ultimate Warrior. Warrior had been away from the wrestling world for a couple years by this time, having parted ways from the WWF for the third, and what was thought to be the final time.

Bischoff's theory on this was to have, what he thought to be, an epic rematch between Hulk Hogan and Warrior from their match at *Wrestlemania VI*. I guess Bischoff thought it was a match that everyone wanted to see.

I will give credit to where credit is due, it wasn't a terrible idea. They're both icons and a match between the two again didn't seem like too bad of a plan, as long as it was executed well...which this one was not.

Warrior was given all creative control and with Hogan also having creative control, it made for an unbelievable mess. Warrior's first appearance on *Nitro* was like a train speeding down the track towards a dead end without stopping.

Him being there definitely wasn't the problem because he got an amazing reaction when he first walked out. However, about five minutes into his promo, you realized that it had already gone two or three minutes too long.

Warrior was always best at shorter promos that had a lot of wordplay but when it stretched too long, it lost its luster and unfortunately that's what his debut suffered from.

Warrior's ideas for the storyline between him and Hogan were very outlandish but I don't think they were as far out there as many believed. They fit his character and what he wanted his character to be. None of it was truly new either, the whole appearing and disappearing tricks were done by characters like Undertaker and Kane long before Warrior debut in WCW.

The story had Warrior creating his own faction to combat the NWO called the OWN, One Warrior Nation. The storyline actually didn't really bother me so much as some of the bits did. I thought the storyline, in general, was fine but needed to be executed properly to work.

The only bit that I felt was executed perfectly out of the entire rivalry was on September 7, 1998. Warrior was set to face The Giant in a steel cage match and before the match could start, smoke filled the ring and when it cleared, the Giant was on the ground with Warrior sitting in a chair casually. That was one of the best-executed bits I had ever seen Warrior pull off and was the only bit that I can remember working perfectly in this rivalry.

For as many good moments as the rivalry had, it had double the share of bad moments. Warrior's WCW debut aside, a lot of his ideas, while suiting his character, just didn't look good on television, and probably looked worse when watching them in person.

During *Nitro*, Hogan and Bischoff were in the back and Hogan looks into a mirror and sees Warrior. The entire segment was meant to be set up to where only Hogan could see Warrior in the mirror. There was one problem, everyone watching on television could see him too. The only person pretending not to see him in the segment was Bischoff, which made it turn out to be a big joke. It would have been a joke regardless but might have worked a little better if they had tried to play it off more effectively.

This brings me back to the problem that I stated earlier, while all of this was going on, Goldberg would be set to face Diamond Dallas Page. This was actually a pretty good match up and setup because it was two babyfaces going one-on-one. However, we rarely saw the build up for this because it took a backseat to

Hogan and Warrior, despite being the main event at *Halloween Havoc.*

Halloween Havoc would take place on October 25, 1998. The event actually did have a good card. In fact, two of the matches from the main event card were some of my favorites from WCW period. There was Goldberg vs. Page and then you had Bret Hart vs. Sting. Hart and Sting were two of the best to go head-to-head with each other. Hart had the technical skill, while Sting had the speed and charisma for the match. This was a match that deserved to be placed above Hogan and Warrior, but as fate usually had it with WCW, it was placed below it.

After a tremendous match between Hart and Sting, we were led into Hogan vs. Warrior. After two really good entrances by both icons, the match began and all inconsistencies ensued. Truth be told, the match is not as bad as it has been described over the years. In fact, they tried to recreate a lot of stuff from their match at *Wrestlemania VI.* There was just one problem, this was 1998 and the fans were much different and older by this point. This led to a pretty lifeless match, and the lack of support in the crowd didn't help it.

While the timing of both men was off, the match was mainly hurt, performance-wise, by its ending. Hogan has admitted to planning the ending and messing it up. The idea was to have the Warrior make a comeback completely blind. It's actually an idea that fits the Warriors character very well. He was very over the top, so why not have an over the top ending to their match?

The match had already been running on long by the time they got to their planned ending, due to a lot of mistimed maneuvers, but apparently, no one told them that in the ring. Hogan got out a wad of flash paper and a lighter. As he was trying to light it up to throw it in Warrior's face, the lighter would not light. Hogan, out of desperation, still threw some of the flash paper at Warrior even though it wasn't lit. Warrior reacted as though he had been hit, but as luck should have it, the rest of paper in Hogan's hand lit up at the last second and burst back into Hogan's face.

To the commentator's credit, they tried to play it off, and they did the best they could. The rest of the match was just a laugh-fest after that. Horace was brought out by Bischoff and they quickly ended the match from there with Horace hitting Warrior in the back with a chair and Hogan getting the victory.

As strange as this might sound, I actually always loved the ending to this match because of the absurdity of it. You could see the anger on Bischoff's face when he ran out. It was then that you knew something had gone wrong.

Due to the match running far too long, the main event between Goldberg and Page didn't have a lot of air time. WCW (mainly Bischoff) has been criticized for not informing the network of the mistake and asking for more time. WCW and WWF had been guilty of this plenty of times before but still managed to get the network's permission to run longer.

For whatever reason, WCW either forgot to ask or thought they could make the scheduled time limit. As a result, the match between Goldberg and Page was cut off halfway through; resulting in thousands upon thousands of people losing the match they had paid to see.

Bischoff, to his credit, knew that it was a mistake on their part, so he scheduled for the match to be rerun on *Nitro* the next night. This is one mistake where I stand completely behind Bischoff's decision and don't agree with the rest of the fans who complained. Many fans complained that the match that they paid to see was now being shown for free the next night and demanded a refund for the entire event, which WCW obliged and refunded a few days later.

I don't agree with the refund because technically, the fans paid for a two-hour event, all of which they saw except for the last ten minutes. I felt that Bischoff made the right decision to show the match the next night but should not have had to refund anybody. It's much like a movie that you pay to see, you're allowed to get your money back after a few minutes, but after that you're stuck. WCW should have treated it like that.

Unfortunately, with the ratings no longer in their favor and not wanting to lose any more viewers, they complied with the demands.

Getting back on topic, Warrior would appear on *Nitro* after Halloween Havoc but would disappear after that. According to Hogan, they were negotiating with Warrior to keep the storyline going and to have a rematch to make up for the horrible match they had. Only Hogan's side of the story has been disclosed on Warrior's departure, which depicted Warrior asking for far too much and WCW rejecting his request.

It's tough to believe anybody in the wrestling world and Hogan is one of the toughest. Especially when you consider the fact that Hogan had already demanded so much and had never been rejected once. Warrior would disappear from the wrestling world for several years after that, but would not remain silent about WWF, WCW, and would definitely not remain silent on Hogan.

He might be viewed as one of the oddest characters to come out of wrestling, but you have to admit, most of what Warrior has said about wrestling over the years made a lot of sense.

Chapter XIX
WWF's Good and Bad Angles, Invades WCW

With WCW tripping over their own feet, it was really up to WWF to take advantage. They had a lot of creative highs going on during this time. The Austin/McMahon rivalry was going strong, Degeneration-X was reaching levels of popularity that weren't expected of them, and their mid-card was starting to come to life.

That's not to say they weren't messing up either. Their Woman's Division, which they had just reformed, was a train wreck with Sable as the lead female on the show, and their Light Heavyweight Division was a poor copycat of WCW's Cruiserweight Division.

Also, a few of their characters from previous years were falling flat. The character of Goldust, who was one of my favorites, was led to absolutely nowhere in 1998. Legendary tag team, The Road Warriors (Legion of Doom in WWF) were given little to no room in the tag team division and were given the most bogus storyline ever.

I'll touch base on this for a little bit before I move on to our next subject. The Road Warriors had an on and off relationship with the WWF up until that point. While their first tenure with the company was very memorable, their second tenure was a miserable mess.

The WWF had no problem humiliating them as a tag team and almost erasing their legacy completely, or so it seemed to us fans. It obviously wasn't too big of a deal to Animal and Hawk because they agreed to do it.

After going off-screen for a couple months after they were embarrassed by another tag team, The New Age Outlaws (Jesse James and Billy Gunn), they returned to the WWF at *Wrestlemania XIV* with a new look and Sunny as their manager. I actually really liked their return because it made them look like the dominant tag team they were built up to be.

As 1998 rolled on, the WWF went back to humiliating them to a certain degree, but in a different way. Hawk (Michael Hegstrand) was suffering from real-life problems; he was addicted to drugs and was an alcoholic at the time. The WWF found it fit to bring his real-life problems into a storyline.

Not only was this tasteless from the start, but they kept it going for a couple months. The storyline involved Hawk no longer being able to handle himself completely as a member of the team. They had just recruited a new member of the team, Puke (Darren Drozdov) to fill in for Hawk.

The storyline continued with Hawk showing signs of disapproval of Puke but continuing to show up to matches intoxicated.

The WWF decided to conclude the story with Hawk climbing on top of their Titantron, and being pushed off by Puke. They then showed a shadow going down the screen, to give the impression that Hawk fell.

This storyline was done without the consent of Hawk or Animal but they were given no choice due to their contracts. The week after, instead of apologizing to viewers after so much bad press from the angle, the WWF continued it by Puke saying that he enabled Hawk's addiction in order to get rid of him.

It was one of the most tasteless storylines that I've ever seen pulled off by the WWF (even as the WWE now), and that says a lot.

After *Wrestlemania*, WWF was starting to get bolder in their attempts to compete with WCW. Up until then, they hadn't really acknowledged WCW since 1996, when they did the *Billionaire Ted* skits. However, as the war was getting more and more personal between the two companies, McMahon decided to play hardball for the first time.

On April 27, 1998, *Raw* and *Nitro* would only be a few miles away from each other as *Raw* would be held in Hampton, Virginia, and *Nitro* in Norfolk, Virginia. Some have claimed that WCW did this in order to play dirty with WWF or vice versa. It's tough to really say, none of us were in charge of the books for either company, so for all we know, it could have been a simple booking coincidence.

Raw was set to be live this night because WWF was just coming off another pay-per-view from the previous night, *Unforgiven*. However, WCW was pre-empted this night, so it is not considered an official ratings competition night for the two shows. McMahon on the other hand did feel like making this night a competition in another way.

Since the shows were so close to each other, McMahon decided to send his biggest stable, Degeneration-X, to go crash WCW's party at Norfolk. He quite literally had them show up outside of the arena, driving a military vehicle with a cannon loaded on top of it. In this segment, they fired the cannon, signaling the start of the war.

It was surreal to watch a WWF broadcast and see them at an arena with WCW's *Nitro* advertisement on it. They would drive around the arena and shout out to Kevin Nash and Scott Hall (real-life friends of DX members Triple H and Sean Waltman).

One moment has been marked as very significant for the segment and that's when DX was approaching one of the garage doors to the arena and WCW shut it.

Triple H has stated that before the segment was due to take place, while they were planning he had asked, "What if WCW allows us into the building?" McMahon replied that they should go in because what are fans going to watch, the show with no one on it or the show with everyone on it?

It was a valid point, but it could have been a problem too. The segment was filmed at a very unusual moment for WCW because it was one of the very few times that *Nitro* was not live. They were actually taped this night due to pre-emption and the episode was being taped at the time that DX arrived. Also, the segment was actually filmed before *Raw* was live on the air. They had to film this well beforehand to make sure that everything went smoothly and without a problem (they could have been arrested, jumped by WCW wrestlers or both). This was because if something went wrong, they couldn't air it.

That leads into Bischoff's answer to that question as well. He's been asked several times why he didn't let them in, and his answer has always been that he had no idea that it was going on.

That is actually a very true statement because it's been proven that at the time of DX's Invasion he was in the ring cutting a promo. He's stated countless times that if he had known, he would have let them in.

The reason why I stated that Vince McMahon's answer could have been a problem is because if Bischoff had let them in, pre-emption or no pre-emption, it could have attracted viewers to WCW's taping of *Nitro*, which was aired the following day. So overall, it's really tough to say whether letting DX in would have favored the WWF or WCW, it could have gone either way.

After this had happened, it was clear to fans watching, that this was actually a battle. It was no longer just a one-sided affair; it was a fight between these two companies.

Chapter XX
Bret Hart and WCW

Bret Hart's tenure with WCW could probably be a book on its own. Bret Hart entered into WCW on December 15, 1997, a little over a month after his fallout with Vince McMahon and the WWF. WCW had built up his debut, but I think that was a sign that WCW didn't quite know what they were doing with him.

Hart had signed a very lucrative three-year contract with them for two and a half million dollars per year. The contract boasted a far lighter schedule than WWF's and gave him a certain amount of creative control. However, things sort of fell off the rails from the start because Hart was no longer under contract with the WWF after *Survivor Series*.

Some have stated it would have been better to introduce him sooner than they did. They obviously wouldn't have introduced him the next night because Hart was still reeling from the effects of *Survivor Series*, but they could have done it the following week, which would have been perfect.

From my standpoint on it, debuting him the week after would have been the smartest move ever. This was the night that McMahon did his famous interview, giving his side of the story on what happened in Montreal. This was a taped *Raw*. WCW clearly knew the results of all of *Raw's* taped shows, so they clearly knew that this interview was taking place.

If they had introduced Hart on this night, and he gave his side of the story, it could have been a humongous ratings surge for them, because McMahon's interview did win WWF the quarter hour, it didn't win them the night, but it won them that small segment of the night. If WCW had Hart on the show, it could have even prevented that.

Hart's debut was lukewarm at best, taking a month to bring him in I think hurt his momentum, which he had a lot of when he left the WWF. As I stated earlier, they brought him on to be part of the Hogan/Sting angle. During their match at *Starrcade*, Sting was supposed to be screwed out of the match and Hart was supposed to restart the match and Sting would win from there. Again, the match didn't end as planned but it really didn't concern Hart after the match took place.

Hart remained out of action for his first month with WCW and was more of a face for promos. This was because he had a sixty day no-compete clause on his contract with the WWF. The no-compete clause for wrestling is similar to other sports contracts. This means that a superstar cannot compete for a rival promotion for a certain period of time, the minimum usually stands at thirty days and is as high as sixty days, and Hart got the max.

After his no-compete clause ran out, he entered into a feud with Ric Flair. The storyline was simple and it was the fact that both of them considered themselves the best wrestler of all-time (not an entirely fabricated story) and they needed to see who was best.

They had a really good match at *Souled Out*, and it was a great first match for Hart in WCW. Things kind of tapered off a bit from there where Hart turned heel by associating himself with the NWO. This element of Hart's tenure with the company I didn't enjoy at all, mainly because he would have to resort to heel tactics to win or lose his matches. For matches like his first match with Chris Benoit, it just didn't work. Having two great wrestlers end their match with interference on Hart's behalf just didn't help the match at all.

Something was a bit strange about Hart's first year with WCW. He wrestled for lower card titles but didn't wrestle for the WCW title. Some people have predicted that Hogan had something to do with Hart's heel turn in WCW, because as a heel, he could not contend for his title.

Others have argued that Hart did it to himself because of his creative control. This is actually fairly untrue. Hart had a certain amount of creative control but not one-hundred percent of it. Hogan, on the other hand, had almost full creative control over his character, as did others. So in many ways, Hart actually had less say than most of the other legends that were on the roster. This meant that Hart's decision could be overridden by another with more say than him. Obviously, Bischoff had more say than him, but in some way Hogan had more say than Bischoff because of his contract.

Hart would win WCW's secondary singles title, the United States Championship, eight months into his stint with the company against Diamond Dallas Page. His first reign was kind of weird because he would lose it three weeks later to Lex Luger, only to regain it back on that week's edition *Thunder*.

Hart's character would continue down a weird path as he would fake a face turn and align himself with Sting, only to turn against Sting and become a heel again weeks later. So, there were a lot of strange things going on with Hart's character, and having seen the way Hart's character was handled in the WWF, it was unquestionable that Hart wasn't behind a lot of the planning.

One really interesting interview that McMahon did for Hart's biography in 2010 had him stating that he was scared that they wouldn't know what to do with him, and how he saw that those fears were well-founded. They certainly were as Hart seemed to be there just to do random things with no real motive to them, which is sad considering this was a guy that was main eventing in sold out arena's for WWF and was forced to kind of play second fiddle to the main event guys in WCW.

Another popular saying from McMahon is him stating that if he were in WCW, he could build the entire franchise around Hart and make it work. It's definitely not a fabrication as he built the WWF around Hart for an extended period of time.

I think the biggest issue was that Hart was clustered around a bunch of aging legends that didn't like having him there. True, Hart was not the youngest guy around either, but he could still wrestle with the best of them, which to me, put him way above Hogan, Savage, and Nash.

To WCW's credit, they put Hart in a great rivalry with Sting in the latter part of 1998 that culminated at *Halloween Havoc*. They had a great match and it was one of my favorites from that event.

I think that was the part that really hurt about Hart's tenure with WCW for that first year. He was someone that could still wrestle like no one else. He was in his forties and could hold his own in the ring but wasn't really moving up the ladder to where Hogan was. That first year almost felt like Hogan's last year with WWF, where Hart was being held down by the screwed up system that Hogan rode on.

When 1999 rolled along, Bischoff wanted to make Hart's role in WCW more prominent. He was in desperate need of a new face for the company because the more established WCW faces were not having the same effect as they were before and there really was no other established older wrestler on the roster that could help escalate younger wrestlers other than Hart, while also being a face for the company.

Bischoff had a pretty good idea, Hart was going to be gone on injury, he had suffered a torn groin muscle in a match against Dean Malenko. To give him a good send-off, they would make it look like he quit WCW. Hart would come out on camera on March 29, 1999, in Toronto, Canada and completely put down Ric Flair and Hulk Hogan, giving what appeared to be a very legit promo because it was well documented how they all hated each other.

He would then call out Bill Goldberg.

Goldberg would come out and Hart would coerce him into spearing him. Goldberg would spear him and Goldberg would be rendered unconscious. Hart would get up and reveal that he had a metal plate under his jersey and would get back on the microphone and tell Bischoff that he quit.

This was my absolute favorite promo from Hart during his time at WCW. Hart brought so much emotion to the promo and his fake reaction to Goldberg's spear was hilarious.

Hart would then take time off for surgery. He was only supposed to be gone for two months. He did several interviews to make his departure from WCW look legit. He was then supposed to go on the Jay Leno show to promote his return when fate struck.

On May 23, 1999, Hart's younger brother Owen fell ninety feet performing a stunt entrance into the ring. I'll get to this full story later but to make a long story short, Owen passed away on that night. All plans with Bret Hart's storyline were canceled at that point and he took an additional four months off.

One of the most memorable promos that Hart ever gave for WCW was, unfortunately, a very real one and that was the one he gave to the fans shortly after Owen passed. It was a sad segment to hear because it was one of those moments where it really touched you but all of us wished that moment didn't have to happen and that Owen would still be with us.

Hart would return to WCW on September 13. Because he had intended to push Hart before his absence, Bischoff wanted to continue the plan and proceeded to push Hart more and more on television. It eventually led to a tournament for the then vacant WCW World Heavyweight Title. The tournament would progress through several episodes of *Nitro* and would end at their pay-per-view, *Mayhem*. Hart would face Chris Benoit in the finals in one of the best matches Hart ever put on in WCW. Hart and Benoit had unbelievable chemistry in the ring and their fifteen-minute match was some of the best fifteen minutes that I've ever seen in wrestling.

To see Hart hold up that championship belt was very cool. It was nice to see him finally being acknowledged in the way that he should have been from the start in WCW.

According to rumors, Hart's reign was supposed to last for a while, with most saying up to a year and it would have been well-deserved. He would briefly win the Tag Titles with Goldberg on December 7 but would lose them the following week.

Fate would strike another crushing blow on December 19, 1999, at WCW's annual event, *Starrcade*. Hart was set to face Goldberg in a championship match. In the middle of the match, Goldberg would land a hard mule kick to the side of Hart's head, giving him a severe concussion.

When watching the match, you could see very clearly that something was wrong. Hart looked slightly wobbled after Goldberg's kick. He kept going, but you knew that he was off-balance for the rest of the match. The match would end with Hart winning controversially.

Hart would vacate the title and would actually continue to wrestle for a short while after that, regaining the title at some point, but it was clear when you watched his matches that he couldn't quite do it anymore. Something was definitely wrong with him and it was noticeable on television.

Hart would announce his retirement in October of 2000 after several months of being off television. According to sources, WCW terminated their contract with Hart by FedEx, falling one month shy of finishing their three-year deal.

If I could sum up Hart's tenure with WCW, it would be disappointing. While the latter part of his WCW career was very good as they would finally utilize him to his full capacity, it just wasn't the same. I think Bret Hart got himself into a company that might have had good intentions but had too many political forces that were there to keep guys like him down.

I think if WCW had used him to his full potential from the start, they might have had a game saver for them, and maybe Hart's wrestling fate would have been much different. We can't really say, for all we know, it might have wound up the same, but it's all in the past now and in the past it shall remain.

Chapter XXI
WWF's Creative Highs and Lows, Owen Hart's Death

The WWF rolled through 1998, appearing to be on a creative high that had no limits. As 1999 began to roll around, WWF and WCW were achieving ratings numbers that were thought to be impossible for wrestling. The combined audience for the shows was over ten million viewers, which were some of the highest ratings that wrestling had seen since the 80s'.

There was a problem, the wrestling business was becoming so big that it fit right into Paul Heyman's quote again, "It was an inflated bubble that had to burst." Wrestling was growing at such a fast rate and it was pretty tough to keep up with some weeks.

To be honest, while WWF was considered to be the better product to watch at the time, it was still doing a lot of the things that I felt were a bit outlandish. I thought the whole Ministry angle with the Undertaker was kind of weird and when it combined with the Corporation, it was just overblown.

Early 1999 I thought was left open for both companies to take advantage of because it didn't feel like either company was excelling at the early part of the year. The WWF's start to 1999 was very slow; they really were relying on the Austin/McMahon rivalry to push them forward. They did have a great rivalry eventually start with The Rock and Mick Foley, but their mid-card was kind of in flux. So they were really leaning on main event talent early on.

Factions like Degeneration-X and the Oddities were growing stale and many superstars such as Kane, Ken Shamrock, Edge & Christian, and more were in-between storylines and were going nowhere early in the year, so WWF's position was a vulnerable one as they were building up their storylines for the year because a lot of them took a while to materialize.

I think a lot of this had to do with their huge run in 1998. They ran with so much speed in 1998 that it left them sort of flat for the start of 1999. I think if Austin and McMahon or Rock and Mick Foley had not been as good as they were, the beginning of the year would have been a dud for them.

Speaking of Rock and Foley, this leads me to a very significant point of the ratings war between the two companies. On January 4, 1999, WWF would air a taped *Raw* from December 29. The taped *Raw* would be the night that Foley won the WWF Championship. On this night, *Nitro* was promoting a live rematch between Goldberg and Kevin Nash.

The rematch stemmed from the match they had at their annual event, *Starrcade* in 1998. The match generated a negative response as it brought an end to Goldberg's undefeated streak, and many felt that the streak ended at the wrong time and to the wrong person.   Many who saw the event thought that it was Kevin Nash playing around with his creative control and trying to put himself on top.

The rematch between Goldberg and Nash was highly anticipated and had *Nitro* ahead in the ratings for most of the night. A lot of fans, including me, thought it was WCW's attempt to make up for the *Starrcade* match.

During the event, despite having the lead, Bischoff gave orders to his commentator, Tony Schiavone, and had him give the results away for WWF's main event. After making this announcement, over six-hundred thousand viewers switched over to the WWF, giving WWF the victory that night.

Bischoff's orders on this night didn't make a lick of sense because they had a surefire winning night on their hands and just gave away their chance at winning.

Granted it wouldn't have mattered because they screwed fans out of a chance to see the rematch anyway because they created a stupid plot twist where Goldberg was arrested and it turned into a comedic match between Hogan and Nash, which resulted in Hogan poking Nash in the chest and getting the win. Fans have dubbed the event *The Finger Poke of Doom*. It was quite clear that WCW only promoted the match to gain viewers and nothing else.

WWF wasn't innocent either. The lack of mid-card storylines had them resulting to dangerous stunts. One event that sticks out very well was the *Royal Rumble*. It was The Rock facing Mick Foley in a rematch from their match on *Raw*, and they went extremely overboard.

I was very happy to see Foley as champion but his match with The Rock at *Royal Rumble* was just an attention seeking match and didn't have to be. During the match Foley and Rock were battling in the crowd and above the electrical equipment for the event. Rock would knock Foley down into the equipment causing the lights to go out. They would then proceed with one of the most violent conclusions to a match that I've ever seen. Foley would take an unprecedented eleven chair shots to the head and this would lead to the finish of the match with Foley supposedly saying "I Quit". I say supposedly because it would be revealed that Foley's words were stolen from a previous recording and that Foley hadn't said "I Quit" at all and was screwed out of the title.

So, when it comes right down to it, WWF was just as guilty of seeking attention as WCW, the only difference was they did it in different ways, and in my opinion, neither way was smarter than the other.

As the ball began rolling with 1999, both companies would go in separate directions. WWF tried to expand their mid-card with storylines that took up as much television time or more than the upper card, while WCW had rehashed the already stale NWO storyline.

As 1999 progressed, the ratings steadily began to decline for WCW and climb for WWF. I honestly believe that both products had their flaws but WCW's problems were becoming more and more apparent on-screen. In just a five-month span, the ratings went from a 5.0 rating to just above 3, so it was a very drastic change in a short amount of time.

There was a moment in 1999 that I thought would cripple the WWF. On May 23, the world of wrestling was rocked by the death of Owen Hart. As I stated earlier, Hart was set to make a special entrance, where he was lowered down to the ring from the rafters of the arena. The harness that he was wearing was released by accident, and he fell to his death.

The incident has never been aired as it happened while a promo for his match was being shown on television. The description that fans have stated about the incident was that he screamed all the way down, hit his head on the turnbuckle and went limp in the ring. Many fans in attendance thought it was part of the show.

A little under a half-hour later, Jim Ross let the viewing audience know that Hart had passed away from the fall. It was honestly one of the most heartbreaking things on the face of the earth because he was still so young and at the top of his game in the ring.

When it was learned that Hart had passed, all of the viewing audience at home thought that the show would be stopped. McMahon ordered that the show continue. This led to a media frenzy and rage from the fans. I myself was disgusted with McMahon's decision. When fans in attendance learned of the death after leaving that night, some gave interviews stating their disgust.

So many people have stated that they believe that McMahon let the show go on, not to be respectful to Hart's memory, but to avoid having to give refunds for the event. I'm going to be honest; I would not put it past McMahon to do that.

The very next night, they dedicated the

entire *Raw* episode to Hart. It was one of the first tribute shows that they ever did and it just came off bad for the WWF. Owen Hart's tribute left everyone with a really sour taste in their mouths unlike future tribute shows, and I think a lot of it had to do with the circumstances surrounding it.

Hart's family, including Bret, blamed the WWF for his death. Hart was reluctant to do the stunt and it's been rumored that he only did it after being pressured by McMahon to do so, which doesn't sound unlike McMahon.

After the incident, lawsuits were filed against the WWF, with Hart's family focused primarily on McMahon. A ton of bad press hit the WWF and it was thought that the incident would cripple the company, which was still private at the time. McMahon was being looked at as a murderer to some degree by the Hart family.

From my standpoint, I thought the incident would damage the WWF's reputation and pro wrestling's reputation to the point where it would show up deeply in the ratings. I was expecting the ratings to dip badly for the WWF. Fortunately for them, all it did was give them a huge level of bad press that would literally last for months and would sporadically reappear whenever something bad would happen in the company.

Honestly, the best tribute that was ever done for Owen Hart was the match that Bret Hart and Chris Benoit had on October 4, 1999, when WCW aired *Nitro* from the same venue where Owen Hart had passed away, the Kemper Arena. It was a great match and really emotional to watch.

Chapter XXII
Bischoff Loses Control, Vince Russo Steps In

As 1999 rolled along, Time Warner continued to take a firm grasp onto WCW. For Eric Bischoff, it was becoming increasingly more difficult to run WCW under their watch and compete with the WWF's surge in popularity.

Time Warner's order for a family-friendly show was causing WCW to fall well behind the changing times in wrestling as the WWF continued to turn its product more in-line with older audiences, with many being within the teen and adult male demographic, the demographic that WCW used to cater to.

With pressures growing, Bischoff was trying anything to keep the competition going with the WWF, but it was incredibly tough as the roster was being held down by aging superstars with guaranteed money, creative control, and lazy attitudes. These were wrestlers that refused let go of their top spots and were unwilling to let a younger generation of superstars take the company where it needed to be.

Also, budget cuts were beginning to hurt the quality of the programming and the shows stretched budget with *Nitro* and *Thunder* was beginning to show on camera. *Nitro* and *Thunder* had to alter their sets and looks to accommodate the cuts, making the shows look inferior to their competition.

To make matters worse, WCW's creative woes were becoming more noticeable to the audience as the product continued to reuse old storylines and stables to try and stay afloat, instead of creating anything new.

This took a huge effect on WCW's revenues, as ratings, attendance, and buyrates were dropping to disastrous lows. WCW's profits were declining at an alarming rate with the company losing north of five million dollars per month.

Bischoff would make one last ditch effort in the bitter rivalry with WWF. He would make a deal with the legendary rock group, *Kiss*, and have them perform on the show. They were brought on to help promote a new character inspired by them called *The Kiss Demon*. While visually a pretty cool character, it didn't save it from being the dumbest idea that WCW had come up with at that point.

Bischoff also thought that having *Kiss* perform live on *Nitro* would be a ratings hit. Unfortunately, the quarter hour for *Kiss'* performance drew one of the worst quarter-hour ratings in wrestling history.

With WCW appearing to hand WWF their

victories in the ratings, TBS Sports Chief Harvey Schiller decided that WCW was in need of new management and pulled Bischoff into a meeting, and let him know that he would be relieved of his duties.

Bischoff has stated in the past that he was ready to be relieved of his duties at that point. The weight of WCW was really bearing down on him and took this as a good chance for a break. Schiller may have relieved Bischoff of his duties but he didn't fire him, he more or less placed him on the shelf to see if they would ever need him back or not.

Bischoff, who was then listed as President of WCW, was written off-screen and the title of President was stripped away from WCW. Schiller would give control of WCW to Bill Busch. Busch, while hardly known, was actually already part of WCW as Vice President. Since Bischoff was an on-screen character, the involvement of Busch in WCW was hardly mentioned and why his name was rarely written about.

The first thing Busch was self-aware of was that he didn't have a creative mind for wrestling. He would need to bring in a person or two to handle the creative side of the company. Desperate times called for desperate measures and Busch secured a deal with WWF's Head Writer, Vince Russo and his writing partner, Ed Ferrera.

This was a very controversial decision to make because Russo was still under contract with WWF when the deal was signed. Russo and Ferrera backed out of WWF in the middle of several storylines at the time. According to Russo, the decision was made after recent decisions from McMahon that he wasn't happy with, which included the introduction of WWF's Thursday night show, *Smackdown*. The increased workload with the new show was pressuring to Russo, which effectively caused him to seek employment elsewhere.

Russo's reasoning though doesn't make a whole lot of sense, especially when you consider the job he took with WCW. The job pretty much had him doing the same thing. In fact, he signed on to a bigger job because he and Ferrera would be the only ones handling creative for both *Nitro* and *Thunder*. So Russo's reasoning for leaving was already a bullshit story.

There has been a lot of speculation as to how Russo even got the job in the first place. I think a lot of it had to do with Busch's position at the time and WCW's position as well. The company was in a state where something needed to happen fast. Things were quickly becoming bleak for the company.

To top it all off, there weren't a lot of

resources for WCW to use. They needed someone who was inexpensive to them without looking for someone outside of the wrestling circle. They also needed someone who they could look at as a resource for storylines that would help WCW revive its image. Busch saw that in Russo because he viewed him as the guy that saved the WWF in 1998.

While there is some truth to that, the one thing that Busch didn't see was the fact that all of Russo's storylines were being handed to and critiqued by Vince McMahon.

In Russo's defense, I don't think he had any real bad intentions with WCW. I don't think he walked into it and simply said, "I know I can't fix this but I'll join WCW anyway". I think he legitimately wanted to fix WCW and thought he had the proper knowledge to do so.

I think one of the main things that fans tend to overlook and so many within the WWE choose to never mention is that when Russo landed his role in WCW, he was handed a mess. I personally feel that a lot of people within the industry, particularly Bill Busch, expected far too much from Russo and in-turn put so much pressure on Russo to recreate what was done in WWF.

Don't get me wrong, I'm not saying this to

cover up some of Russo's terrible ideas, but he's gone on record and some have actually vouched for him, that when he went to WCW, it was ordered to him to fix the company and do it fast. Busch was under pressure as well. WCW was under heavy surveillance from members of Time Warner, who were taking over Turner Broadcasting more and more and they didn't want WCW at all. So, the only way to keep WCW afloat was to turn things around, because if the company could improve, there was nothing justifiable that Time Warner could do to them, especially if they were earning a profit.

One of Russo's philosophies that was made quite clear on WCW programming was acknowledging the competition on the air. Russo has stated that when you're number one, you shouldn't even point any sort of finger at your competition. However, if you're losing, you have to; you want to show that you're there to fight. I'm all for wrestling programs knocking their competition because I think it's fun to see and shows the realism of the business. However, Russo more or less took jabs this time for personal reasons rather than just for competition. The *Oklahoma* character, among the rest, was one of the lowest things I've ever seen Russo pull off and I was very stunned that Busch allowed that segment to go on.

One of the things I agreed with Russo on was the pushing of younger stars within the company. WCW, even then, had a great lineup of young talent that were great in-ring workers. Russo though wanted to push them right away and immediately phase out the older stars without any sort of notice. I understood his idea but there has to be a transition there in order to make it work, because without a gradual transition, it feels force fed to fans.

The only established stars that Russo seemed to lean on were Jeff Jarrett and Bret Hart, because while they were getting up there in age as well, they were still great in-ring performers and could help push the younger stars and make them look good. I sort of liked the reformation of the NWO with Jarrett and Hart, I thought that was a pretty neat idea in itself, but tragedy did strike as this was cut short by Hart's forced retirement only half a year into the storyline.

While bringing up the younger stars was a great idea, some of Russo's other ideas were just horrendous. The *Piñata* or *Viagra on a Pole* matches were just low brow and unnecessary. I think this all leads back to the same problem that I mentioned earlier, Russo did not have a filter and Busch was not intelligent enough, wrestling-wise, to be that filter. If he had to answer to Time Warner or Turner directly, as Bischoff did, it would have probably been different but there wasn't that option for him.

Russo's solo tenure with WCW would only last mere months as a lame booking idea would get him and his writing partner, Ed Ferrera, suspended. Leading up to WCW's January pay-per-view, *Souled Out* in 2000, a decision was needed to be made for World Champion. WCW's two top performers Bret Hart and Jeff Jarrett were out on injury (Hart's permanent and Jarrett's temporary). Russo had the idea of turning former UFC fighter, Tank Abbott, into the new champion.

I'm not necessarily against former fighters or other athletes being a wrestling champion, as long as they're good wrestlers because they do add a level of legitimacy. There was a problem, Abbott was one of the worst UFC fighters in history. It was because of this reason that wrestling fans did not warm up to him and refused to warm up to him. To add insult to injury, he never showed any level of commitment towards wrestling, appearing as though he refused to improve his skills in the ring.

After Russo presented the idea, he was literally suspended right after. Busch and a few others took over the billing of *Souled Out* and made Chris Benoit champion. Making Chris Benoit champion was one of the smartest moves WCW had made in a very long time. There was another problem, so many years of mistreatment from WCW led to not only Benoit, but Eddie Guerrero, Perry Saturn, and Dean Malenko, leaving WCW only weeks (if not less) after winning the title and appearing on WWE programming immediately.

With no booker or creative lead currently in WCW after Russo's suspension, Busch was forced to reach back out to Bischoff.

Chapter XXIII
WWF's Creative High's

Vince Russo's departure from WWF was surprisingly a good thing in late 1999. WWF sort of needed a shot in the arm in late 1999 because while the company was still successful ratings-wise, they took two big hits in 1999. They would lose two big-named performers that year to injury, they lost The Undertaker to a groin injury (which would also include an arm injury during recovery) and they lost their biggest name, Stone Cold Steve Austin to neck surgery and he would be off screen until late 2000.

The departures forced WWF to lean on two new stars, Triple H and The Rock. They also increased the storylines for their mid-card, which in-turn would be a huge benefit. I consider August-November of 1999 to be WWF's struggling months during that year because Austin's in-ring performances were already slowing down as his knee and neck injuries were starting to take effect, and Undertaker wasn't performing at all. Triple H and The Rock were still building themselves at this time, they were over with the crowd for the most part but weren't quite ready to be on their own without the other two. To add to it, Russo's latter storylines before his departure were not that great.

The very last storyline he was involved in was with Vince McMahon's daughter Stephanie marrying wrestler Test. Throughout 1999, Stephanie McMahon was slowly becoming more and more of a regular on camera but her good girl image on-screen was not playing out with the audience. Russo tried to remedy this in some way with the wedding. The initial idea of the wedding was completely retarded and if it had gone through with just the wedding, it would have been a train wreck.

During the storyline, Russo parted ways with WWF and left the ending to the storyline up in the air. With no ending to the story, WWF's remaining creative team prolonged it by having Stephanie McMahon lose her memory for a few weeks to give them time to find a conclusion. It would be Triple H who would conceive the conclusion of having him marry Stephanie. The storyline concluded with Triple H revealing that he drugged Stephanie and eloped with her behind Test's back, becoming Stephanie's husband and Vince McMahon's son-in-law.

Just like that, they gave a great conclusion to a bad storyline, and that great conclusion gave them the storyline that they would run with for the next year and would lead to some of the greatest moments that

WWF ever produced. This era would be listed as the *McMahon-Helmsley era* and it was great fun to watch on television. It not only helped fill the void of the superstars that were missing but helped establish Triple H and The Rock as two of the WWF's top talents.

The expansion of their mid-card was also a huge help, bringing in Benoit, Guerrero, Malenko and Saturn helped build their mid-card, which was already on the rise. I think the division that was equally as important during this time was their tag teams. Tag team wrestling sort of tapered off for a bit during 1999 but with WWF bringing in newer teams such as The Hardy Boyz, APA, Dudley Boyz, Edge and Christian, and more, they were able to build a division that put on some of the most entertaining matches ever and sometimes eclipsed their main event roster.

WWF just hit a stride that seemed unprecedented for wrestling. They had storylines that were addicting and it always seemed like it was must-see TV. That's not to say all of their ideas were great. One story that will always stick out in my head was Mark Henry and Mae Young. Henry and Young were dating and she eventually became pregnant. While a pregnancy storyline is nothing new, Young was seventy-six at this time, which made for disgusting television.

For the record, I respect the hell out of Mae Young; she's one of the original woman wrestlers and a legend. To her credit, even in her seventies, she wanted to tell a story on television and she actually put on some amazing segments. For instance, even though she was in her late seventies, she took a powerbomb through a table, not once but twice, and the second time was off a stage. So, she might have been old but she was just as big a gamer as the younger roster. I have nothing but respect for her and was heartbroken to hear she had passed away.

However, the storyline with Henry was the absolute worst and it's hard to believe that it wasn't Russo's idea. To end her pregnancy storyline, they had her give birth to a bloody rubber hand...no, just no. So yeah, it wasn't all golden storytelling by WWF during that era either; there were a couple bumps in the road, or in this case, a roadblock.

Chapter XXIV
Bischoff Steps Back In & Bash at the Beach
2000

With Russo suspended, Busch had to make the decision on who to place as head of creative for WCW. With no one else to turn to, he turned to Bischoff. Bischoff was very reluctant to go back to WCW, and understandably so. However, the deal would not just be with Bischoff. Busch wanted Bischoff and Russo to work together as co-heads of the creative team. After a horrible first departure, Bischoff decided to play hardball.

WCW (Time Warner in particular) were trying to buyout out all of the old contracts from everyone on the current roster for cheap flat-rate prices and build new and cheaper contracts. This was a stunt that was meant to try and cut their costs down because some of the contracts were unbelievably high and some of the wrestlers weren't worth that much. Some wrestlers accepted and most refused.

Bischoff was willing to accept the contract buyout. However, he wanted every penny of his existing contract when it was bought out on top of the new contract. Desperate, Busch accepted the deal and Bischoff was brought back on and Russo was also brought back from his suspension. Initially, the creative duo appeared to go very well.

Bischoff did state that he met with Russo and liked him upon meeting him. Russo came off as a very open and good spirited guy. He appeared as someone that Bischoff could work with.

One of the early storylines between the two was the New Blood facing off against the Millionaire's Club, the New Blood being the younger stars and the Millionaire's Club being the older veterans.

This storyline, just based on the concept, should have been a winner from the start. However, it was decided to ruin it quickly and they turned the New Blood into a rehashed version of the NWO, quickly eliminating any credibility the storyline seemed to have from the start, and causing many fans to lose faith in the company's younger stars. Strangely enough, WCW had conceived a pay-per-view for the new group, *New Blood Rising*, and yet the group was disbanded before the event took place.

I firmly believe that the NWO thing was the veterans playing creative control once again. Since most of the veterans refused the contract buyouts, their creative control still remained intact, which pretty much trumped anything that Bischoff and Russo could come up with that they thought would belittle their characters.

It was bullshit, and I have no other way to describe it because the New Blood facing the Millionaire's Club was one of the best ideas conceived in WCW for a while and it was completely ruined. I truly believe that was the storyline that might have generated interest in the company. It's a true shame and it does make many, including me, wonder what the state of the company would have been like had the story continued as originally planned.

To add insult to injury, the professional relationship between Bischoff and Russo was quickly fizzling out as Bischoff and Russo consistently clashed over storylines, which started to show on television as the storylines were never consistent and things constantly seemed to change on a weekly basis.

Financially, the company was in ruins. 2000 would see a colossal loss of sixty million dollars for WCW. Attendance was dwindling to the point where fans would have to be moved and camera angles would have to be changed to make the television audience believe the arenas were sold out. The ratings were still okay by cable standards, but WWF was so far ahead that it would have taken a miracle to catch up in 2000.

The hits kept coming and another big one from that year was David Arquette. Many knew Arquette from the Scream film franchise and being the husband to *Friends* star Courtney Cox. Arquette was starring in a wrestling comedy that year, which was produced by Bischoff called *Ready to Rumble*. The film was actually okay, but that's not the point. To promote the film, it was thought to be a good idea to make Arquette champion.

First of all, the WCW title may not have been with the NWA any longer, but if you were to add that history, it was one of the oldest titles in wrestling with a grander history than even the WWF title. By placing it on a comedy actor with no experience and only using his tenure as the champion for comedy, tarnished everything that title was worth. Arquette himself was against the idea but accepted because he was a wrestling fan.

By this point regardless, the meaning of the title was already steadily being lost. The championship literally changed hands five times already between January and April in that year alone. It finally appeared to be in the hands of someone who deserved it in Diamond Dallas Page but was dropped to Arquette the very next night after he won it and changed hands again twelve days later. It should be noted that even Vince Russo won the title in

September that same year. If the belt wasn't tarnished by then, it sure as hell was when he won it.

To try and save the company again, Bischoff conceived an idea where there would be a controversial storyline over the WCW title. On paper, it actually sounded great. The idea was to have Hulk Hogan face the then WCW champion Jeff Jarrett and have Jarrett lay down for Hogan without Hogan knowing it. The storyline would show that Russo (who was in an on-screen feud with Bischoff at the time) would order Jarrett to lie down and allow Hogan to pin him for the win. Hogan would leave the arena with the belt angry with Bischoff chasing after him and there would be a tournament later on for the vacated title, which another wrestler would win and Hogan would show up after the tournament claiming he's the real champion. This would lead to a champion vs. champion match, which was rumored that Hogan would actually lose.

The initial storyline sounds great and everything was supposed to start at *Bash at the Beach*. The first part went well, Jarrett laid down, Russo threw the belt at Hogan, and Bischoff and Hogan left as planned. However, later on in the same show, Russo came back out and delivered a *shoot* promo on Hogan, insulting him and apparently firing him on camera (though he legally couldn't because of Hogan's contract). Russo went against the whole planned storyline and scheduled a match between Jarrett and Booker T later that night for the title, which Booker T won. Bischoff and Hogan would leave WCW because of Russo's actions, with Hogan even suing WCW.

This story has been told from so many different perspectives and there has been no confirmation whether everything was planned or the first half was planned and the other was not. Russo has claimed that the whole storyline was planned and Hogan was aware of the shoot that he delivered. Bischoff has contested this and said that Russo went into business for himself, with Hogan saying the same.

I have taken Bischoff's side on this primarily because of Hogan's lawsuit. While Hogan's defamation suit was thrown out, he was awarded a lot of money, which was part of their recorded sixty million dollar loss that year. If Hogan hadn't sued, I would have probably sided with Russo, but everything leans towards Bischoff's story and doesn't side with Russo's story at all.

Overall, I was happy to see Booker T as champion, because of the entire roster still there at WCW, he deserved it most. I just wish it had been under better circumstances and that his reign could have been a single long reign and not an on and off reign like so many others at WCW at that time.

Chapter XXV
Bischoff's Attempted Buyout & McMahon's Purchase

Adding to WCW's problems was the merger between Time Warner and AOL. As I stated earlier, when Time Warner merged with Turner Broadcasting, Time Warner was able to slowly make an impact with Turner's company but Ted Turner still reigned supreme as he was the leading stockholder. However, Time Warner's merger with AOL proved to be the nail in the coffin for Turner as he was forced out of his own company due to it. Forcing Turner out had been Time Warner's goal from the get go, so they changed everything about Turner Broadcasting and remodeled the networks in the way they saw fit.

WCW was the first company on their cut list due to its debt. When the merger was announced in January of 2000, it took a year for everything to be finalized, giving WCW time to turn the tide around as best they could in a year time span, because that's all they were literally allowed. Had the company only been slightly in debt, there might have been a chance.

WCW had tried to cut down their cost and save as much money as possible to get them back in the black or as close to it as they could. By February of 2001, they had cut their travel expenses to mainly the Southern United States, no longer traveling the whole country, and performing in smaller arena's that would be easier sellouts. They cut their sets down and as much of production cost as they could. The only thing that was keeping them down was their guaranteed contracts; those were still bleeding a huge whole into their finances.

When none of this worked, AOL Time Warner made the final decision to sell the company. From a business standpoint, it made a lot of sense for them to sell it because it was a huge debt for them and didn't appear to have a turnaround plan. However, it can't be hidden that Time Warner was very underhanded and did everything they could to rid the Turner networks of them completely.

When looking at it in that light, there's that feeling that WCW could have been in the black and still terminated by AOL Time Warner, because it was very apparent that none of them were wrestling fans.

Even though Bischoff had left television and the creative team, he was still under contract. He decided that they were continuing to beat a dead horse and that there was nothing they could presently do with the company that would save it, they would need to take it off television for a while, rebuild it, and rebroadcast it with a new and fresh look. They would take away the house shows and move into a permanent location to film all of their shows, instead of touring (possibly Vegas). Bischoff then decided to put his name in a hat to buy the company.

He partnered up with an entertainment company, Fusient Media Ventures, and came up with an offer of sixty-seven million dollars. They dropped their offer briefly because Vince McMahon put his name in the same hat but was rejected because WWF's then network TNN (which was with Viacom) did not want them owning a show that would likely air on a competing network. After McMahon's deal fell through, Bischoff and Fusient resubmitted their deal.

Thinking that the deal was in the bag, Bischoff went on vacation during the process but received a phone call letting him know that the deal was taken off. AOL Time Warner had appointed a new head of Turner Networks, Jamie Kellner. One of Kellner's first acts was to look at all pending deals going on for his networks. WCW's was the first and largest deal. Kellner was not a wrestling fan and when he talked to Bischoff, he let him know that he had no problem selling WCW's assets, including its trademarks, rings, merchandise deals, and video library to him and Fusient, but he would not give them their timeslot on his network.

Hearing this, Bischoff didn't believe there was any value to WCW without their timeslot and pulled out of the deal. Because the deal no longer included television, this left Vince McMahon wide open to purchase WCW, which he bought for an unbelievably low estimate of three million dollars, a definite low for a company that once made forty million in one year. This, in my view, showed what Kellner and AOL Time Warner thought of WCW and wrestling in general, because even though it was the hottest thing on cable and still the leading show on their network despite its downturn in the ratings, they viewed themselves to be above it.

When it came to Bischoff pulling out, I thought it was a pretty stupid decision on his part. WCW might have been lower in the ratings than it once had been but it was still attracting an audience. With no television deal, he could have bought WCW for a lower sum; in fact, he probably could have bought it out of his own pocket, without Fusient.

During this same time, ECW was offered a deal on the Fox Sports Network, which they refused. ECW was substantially smaller than WCW, which means WCW could have probably gotten the same deal elsewhere or even with Fox as well.

I personally feel that if Bischoff wanted to change the look and feel of the product, switching networks should have been the way to go as well. By sticking with Turner Networks and airing on the same timeslot, the show wouldn't be able to rid itself of the horrible memories of the show it was and would be harder to accept by fans. By switching networks and changing the look of the product as well, you convince everyone that this is going to be different. Whether it's for the good or bad, no one knows, but they're going to check it out to see.

I think Bischoff's reason for pulling away from the deal was for several different issues but there are two reasons at the top of the list. One was the fact that I think he questioned WCW's worth as well. In his mind, I feel that he was nervous that WCW couldn't make it anywhere else but Turner. This brings me to the second reason, he always saw WCW a part of Turner Broadcasting. Bischoff was unbelievably loyal to Ted Turner and Turner was a wrestling fan and loved WCW. I think Bischoff felt that by moving WCW from its longtime home network, it was portraying Ted Turner in some way, even though Turner was not there to answer to or seek advice from.

I could be very wrong on both of those

reasons, but I do find it odd that he pulled away from the deal when it could have been so cheap and probably very easy to get on another network.

The purchase of WCW was finalized on March 23, 2001. WCW was signed on for one final *Nitro* on TNT, which would take place at Club La Vela in Panama Beach, Florida, for WCW's annual *Spring Break-Out* episode of *Nitro*. The event was filled with employees of WWF who were there to take part of the final *Nitro* broadcast and Vince McMahon would appear via simulcast from *Monday Night Raw* to announce the purchase live.

The final *Nitro* was very surreal and emotional to watch because there was a definite level of uncertainty surrounding the show and the roster of WCW. Many fans were under the assumption that both shows would now be on TNN with *Nitro* likely being moved to a new night. However, those within the company were apparently very worried about their jobs as they feared that McMahon would not pick up their contracts.

The final show couldn't have been anymore emotionally satisfying as each match was good for the most part. Seeing Booker T winning the WCW championship on the last show was great, and the main event with Ric Flair and Sting was one of the most emotional matches I think I've ever seen.

I was probably one of many who, for fun, switched channels constantly when Vince McMahon was in the ring during his announcement. It was so weird seeing him on both a WWF broadcast and WCW broadcast.

McMahon stunned everyone, including those in his own company by publicly firing Jeff Jarrett. Jarrett and McMahon were well known for their personal dislike for each other but it was unexpected that he would fire him during his announcement.

It was a surreal announcement by McMahon in general because you couldn't tell whether he was trying to stay in character or was legitimately being himself. You got this overall sense that not even he knew what to make of that very moment.

As big of a moment as it was, I wasn't particularly pleased with McMahon's speech. I know he was happy and I know having WCW gone was a huge weight lifted off of his shoulders, but in his long announcement, he denounced everything that WCW stood for. When he did his thumbs up/thumbs down thing when he wanted the crowd's reaction for who they wanted on the show from WCW, he was quite literally belittling all of the stars he was bringing up.

It's one of those nights where we were all

into it when it happened, but when you look back on it, you realize that Vince McMahon could have handled it a lot better than he did.

Chapter XXVI
The Invasion & Eric Bischoff

With WCW gone, WWF ran for about two months with not much mention of WCW, there were a couple run-ins by Lance Storm and Hugh Morrus, but things officially kicked off on June 24, 2001, when Booker T interfered in the main event at the *King of the Ring* and slammed WWF's top star, Stone Cold Steve Austin through the announce table.

After that, Vince McMahon wanted to test how the audience would react to a WCW match on WWF programming. They scheduled a match between Booker T and Buff Bagwell in Tacoma, Washington. The match would take up the last twenty minutes of *Raw*. It was booed out of the building by the crowd. Looking back on it, it wasn't a terrible match but Buff Bagwell clearly didn't care much for it. Booker T gave a great effort to try and sell the match but Bagwell appeared uninterested. He and Booker T were never truly great together in the ring, so it wasn't a great pairing. They tried it once more the same week on *Smackdown* but the idea was quickly dropped after that.

This led to the start of the *Invasion* angle. The initial angle was supposed to be the babyface wrestlers from WCW facing off against heel McMahon. According to McMahon, they changed it to heel WCW because WWF fans weren't buying the WCW faction as babyfaces. That is possible but I think there's more to it than he says.

ECW was quickly brought into the angle to add depth to the story because the WCW roster that WWF acquired was not nearly big enough to impose a threat on-screen.

This brings me to one of the biggest flaws of this angle and why I think McMahon is not totally honest with how he handled the angle. When McMahon bought WCW, he had placed an offer to buyout contracts to particular superstars. Obviously, some said yes and others said no. One interview that will always stand out to me was an interview with Sting, where he described his offer from the WWF.

Sting said that his interview with McMahon was good and that McMahon was very cordial and pitched a really good offer but that there was a worry on how McMahon would treat WCW wrestlers. One example that Sting gave was a promo on *Smackdown* that featured Booker T and The Rock in a build-up to their match at that years *Summerslam*. Booker T comes out and The Rock stops him from talking and asks the question "Who are you?" Sting felt that in that one line, it had demeaned and diminished a great career that

Booker T had up until that point. I couldn't agree more with Sting.

The Invasion angle came off purely as WWF stomping on both WCW and ECW to prove their superiority. In order for any WCW or ECW wrestler to win their matches, it required two or more of their wrestlers to interfere, where WWF wrestlers could defeat a WCW or ECW wrestler cleanly with no problem.

One particular match that was a standout to me was the match between The Rock and Booker T at *Summerslam*. I always felt that this match should have been a clean match and a way for the WWF audience as a whole to gain a new respect for Booker T, respect that I felt he was owed. The first couple minutes of the match were good but the rest was nothing but interference. I had absolutely no problem with The Rock winning the WCW championship but it was a match that I felt should have been left one-on-one.

With all of that said, it should also be noted that WCW was without a lot of their top players. It's tough to say how the angle would have been if Sting, Goldberg, Flair, the NWO and more had been part of it. With the roster that WWF was able to acquire, with the exception of Booker T and Diamond Dallas Page among others, it was really hard for that roster to compare to Stone Cold, The Rock, Undertaker, Kane and more. So, it could have been more along the lines of McMahon having no choice but to play it that way. In the end, they did have to move a lot of WWF's wrestlers over to WCW and ECW's side to fill it up.

Speaking of which, ECW did have a lot of their top players for the angle but it's tough to pick a standout from that roster other than Rob Van Dam, who was immensely popular when he came into WWF for the angle.

I will admit that the angle was a complete failure for so many reasons but I don't feel comfortable jumping on the bandwagon with so many other fans that said that it was all McMahon's ego. There are so many factors that played into that angle and how it turned out. Sting's interview does play multiple roles in how that angle turned out because it does give us a hint that things might have been different if the bigger names had been a part of it.

After the Invasion angle concluded, WWF went through a great deal of changes leading into 2002. Ric Flair had made his return immediately after the angle had come to an end and would be announced as co-owner of WWF in a new storyline with Vince McMahon.

I have an unbelievable respect for Ric Flair. While I didn't agree with some of his booking decisions in the early stages of WCW, he had such a memorable career and was one of my favorites to watch, especially during the latter part of his career with WWE.

His return would lead to the famous *Brand Extension*, which would split the roster between *Raw* and *Smackdown*. WWF was left with no choice but to do the split because they now found themselves with three companies worth of talent and only two hours per show.

The *Brand Extension* was one of my favorite ideas because it made each show feel important. It made both shows feel like flagship shows and not just a primary or secondary show. Each show had their own set of writers, pay-per-views, and superstars. It was a big deal.

One of my favorite moments of 2002 was seeing Eric Bischoff on *Raw* for the very first time on July 15. It had been built for a couple weeks that Vince McMahon wanted a new *Raw* General Manager to shake up *Raw*. There was some truth behind this because *Raw* was actually down in the ratings compared to *Smackdown*.

Smackdown had, in my view, the better roster of the two shows and a better writer in Paul Heyman. *Raw* was struggling by mid-2002 after their top star, Stone Cold Steve Austin legitimately walked out of the company, leaving the show sort of in disarray.

Jim Ross had initially reached out to Bischoff sometime before this, which he rejected. When they were coming up with the new General Manager angle, it would be Vince McMahon to call Bischoff personally to provide him the offer of returning to wrestling to be the storyline General Manager of *Raw*.

Bischoff has stated that it didn't take long for him to accept McMahon's offer and fully know that they could work together.

WWE did a great job keeping the surprise hidden from fans...until the night it happened. I always felt that Bischoff's surprise entrance was ruined by him walking in on an interview with Booker T in a backstage segment before he walked out on stage.

Looking beyond that, it was a great debut for Bischoff, and seeing him and McMahon hug on camera was unbelievably strange. I consider that moment between the two of them as quite literally the end of the *Monday Night Wars*. While I know it had ended on television over a year before this, seeing that there was no personal rivalry between the two of them said a lot, so I consider that the true end.

Chapter XXVII
Wrestling as it Stands Now

Wrestling has continued to go back and forth on being extremely good to insanely bad. Since WCW's demise there's been a lot missing from wrestling and unfortunately, that void has been really present over the last few years. Not only did WWF lose a battle that cost them their name, now going under the WWE name, but the WWE's roster has consistently been strained under the pressure of them being the only big dog in town.

While the lack of competition wasn't felt early on when WCW went out of business, things slowly started to decline in 2004 and has continued to slowly decline more since then.

Eric Bischoff actually made a good point on Vince McMahon's DVD, *McMahon*. He stated that he felt that the lack of competition wasn't good and that it hurt the business. I think that statement is very true and it was very easy to see the WWE struggling without that competition, especially around 2004 and from that point forward.

I know that TNA is also out there as well and I was all for it when the company opened its doors. TNA however, slowly turned itself into the WCW that we saw in its later years and it's sad. The company had a great deal of potential that was squandered on poor booking decisions and resorting to older wrestlers to carry their show.

If I had to rate the current product of WWE, and I'm talking about the product as of November 26, 2016, I would rate it fair to mediocre. I would say today's product is fair at best. I think it's a product that's really struggling to find its place in the world and doesn't quite know where to go from here.

The WWE is constantly referring back to the old days and has had a tough time moving forward. Unfortunately, it's also been tough for them because a good chunk of its fan base won't allow them to move forward.

The birth of social media has been damning to the wrestling business and so many other businesses as well. Fans always voice their opinions on social media and a lot of it sends the worst mixed messages, which I think contributes to WWE's confusion on where to take their product.

When I look at the product today, I see a company that has tremendous potential. The WWE's current roster is one of the best rosters I think they've had in a long time. I think if the WWE and fans, in general, can let go of the past and accept it as the past, it can be a great product again. The seeds are already planted, it's just a matter of everyone stepping aside and letting them grow.

Do I think that we'll ever see a rivalry like WWF and WCW again? I think it's possible. There are a lot of great independent circuits out there that I think have the potential to grow bigger. My money is on Ring of Honor. ROH is one of the best smaller promotions out there and I think the sky is the limit for them. I would love to see them compete against WWE.

Wrestling evolves like any other business out there. Where that evolution takes us, I have no idea. Only time will tell where wrestling will be several years from now. We'll just have to wait and see.